INSIGHT

THE BUSINESS, LAW, AND ETHICS OF THE FASHION AND MODELING INDUSTRIES

....

KAITLIN PUCCIO, ESQ.

BENT FRAME
PUBLISHING

Bent Frame Publishing
NEW YORK, NY

Publisher's Note: Names, places, scenarios, and incidents are
a product of the author's imagination for the purposes of
concept illustration. Any resemblance to actual people, living
or dead, or to businesses, companies, events, institutions,
situations, or circumstances, is purely coincidental.

This book is not meant to be construed as legal advice.

www.bentframepublishing.com

Insight/ Kaitlin Puccio.
ISBN 978-1-7368303-2-1
Library of Congress Control Number: 2024948425

For You

INTRODUCTION

....

The modeling industry is largely unregulated. There are few laws in place to protect models, and the laws that do exist are generally not enforced. Further, a vast majority of educational institutions that offer fashion industry courses focus on traditional fashion law. That is, they offer classes in intellectual property (copyrights and trademarks), licensing, sustainability, retail, and similar, but they leave out modeling contracts—often because the classes are taught by in-house lawyers for fashion brands and the focus of their work generally does not reach the modeling side of fashion.

Many students graduate from law school without ever having seen a contract. For those who aspire to represent models, not only do they need to understand contracts, but they also need to understand how the evolution of the modeling industry has influenced the peculiar way in which modeling contracts are written.

There are not many resources for models, and there are not many fashion lawyers who focus on the modeling industry. Those who do often do not understand the inner workings of the industry, and they read modeling contracts as if they were any other type of contract. Most fashion and entertainment lawyers who do want to learn about modeling contracts don't know where to look for more information, or find that the information available to them is lacking. As a result, models will enter into oppressive contracts that do not reflect the realities of the industry, and oftentimes will leave the industry prematurely after being mistreated by their agencies.

There is much discussion in fashion about sustainability and ethics as applied to garment workers, but there is less discussion about ethics as applied to models. Why? While there is some general surface knowledge that models are sometimes mistreated, the depth of the issue is widely misunderstood. Industry norms have become the law, and the actual law has been disregarded. Model advocates—often former models—have not been trained to parse legal language, and policymakers have no understanding of how the industry functions. This knowledge gap results in well-intentioned flourishes of the political pen having no real-world effect.

I was a model. I dealt with the industry, and with lawyers who didn't understand the industry. And with contracts that were oppressive, and with agents who didn't understand what the terms of their own contracts meant. I never actively decided that I would stop modeling, but I did refuse to sign several representation contracts, and I was fine with the idea that I might not work as much without an agent.

I did not become a lawyer thinking that I would represent models. But after having been generously offered two contractual atrocities by two different agencies—and turning down what would seem to an outsider to be huge career opportunities but which were in reality opportunities to find myself in enormous debt to these agencies—I decided to start.

I cannot change the industry myself. I cannot change laws and I cannot change people's ethics. But I can change the geography of the knowledge gap. I can start to fill in the crevasse, or at least build a bridge over it. And if more people are able to walk freely between both sides—understanding just enough about both the world of modeling and the laws that govern it—then the industry might start to change.

This book does not present the entirety of the applicable law nor a full ethical analysis of the industry. Rather, it provides enough information for models to understand the types of questions they should be asking, what they are getting themselves into when they decide to pursue a career as a model, and the extent to which they are their own protector in the industry.

If you are a model—or an actor—you should read this book not as a comprehensive guide, but as a launchpad for educating yourself and setting yourself up properly to have a lasting, fruitful, and enjoyable career. Remember that in addition to educating yourself, you should always talk to a lawyer or career consultant to help you navigate your career. This book will help you speak their language.

So, let me share some insight...

L A W

....

Your modeling agent may not actually be an agent.

Almost everyone in—and outside of—the fashion and modeling industries refers to model management companies as modeling agencies. One notable exception is in model representation contracts, where the term "agency" appears very deliberately only in limited circumstances. While the law varies by state (and by country), in the larger markets in the United States, generally agencies need to be licensed to procure work—i.e., book jobs—for their models. The laws in California, for example, that apply to talent agencies are very clear. Agents must be licensed to procure work for artists (talent), and models are considered artists. The laws in New York are less overt, but still unequivocal once they are untangled.

The issue in New York is that to figure out what exactly the applicable law is, you need to understand how several seemingly unrelated laws interact with each other and then try to understand how they are meant to apply to modeling agencies. The shortcut is to look at the employment agency license application and the Department of Labor's

Employment Agency Information sheet for new applicants. These documents both specifically mention modeling, which is a clue that New York probably intended for modeling agencies to be licensed. Then you need to look deeper to find the actual laws that state this.

What is often argued, however, is that modeling agencies fit an "incidental exception" to this requirement, which is found elsewhere in New York law, and this effectively makes them "management companies" rather than agencies subject to licensing requirements. This incidental exception essentially means that if a management company does book a job for a model—that is, procures work for the model without a license—it is acceptable as long as it is secondary to the manager's primary purpose of managing the model's career.

This is reflected in New York model representation contracts, which often explicitly state that the company is not a licensed employment agency, and that it agrees to advise and counsel the model on career matters among other things that do not involve booking jobs for the model. The contract sometimes goes as far as stating directly that the management company does not agree to procure work for the model. The company will further protect itself by also including a clause in the contract that essentially says that no conversations or written exchanges count—so any conversation a model has with her manager about the manager booking work is considered to have never happened; the only thing that matters is what is written in the contract, and nowhere in the contract does it talk about procuring work for models.

It is in this sense that modeling contracts do not reflect the reality of the model-manager relationship, and do not, as a result, offer models much protection. These purported "management companies" generally do focus primarily on finding work for their models, and it is commonly and widely accepted and known throughout the industry that this is the purpose of a management company. They are motivated to procure work for their models by a 20% commission—which is the industry standard rather than a codified law—on their models' gross earnings.

Unlike actors, who often work with both a talent manager (adviser) and a talent agent (booker), models generally only work with their model management company; they don't need to search for an additional booking agent because the management company in fact functions as such.

Some agencies are indeed licensed, but they are mainly located in California. Unlicensed New York agencies call themselves management companies and deny that they are agencies in part to avoid certain regulations like commission caps. If they were licensed in New York, they would only be able to take a 10% commission. No such cap exists in California.

How have these so-called "management companies" in New York been able to operate in this manner for so long? They have greatly benefitted from the knowledge gap, which can be illustrated by a brief analysis of the Fashion Workers Act.

The Fashion Workers Act is meant to regulate New York model management companies in order to provide greater protections for models. Models and policymakers alike have high hopes for the Act, and the intention behind it is admirable. But we need to make sure that the individuals putting these protections together understand the complexities and intricacies of existing New York laws as well as the inner workings of the modeling industry, and understand how to interpret them together as a whole, not as separate parts.

It is inarguable that models need greater protections—it would be nice to think that model managers/agents could self-regulate and treat models appropriately, but this is not the reality, and thus imposing regulations makes sense. However, the Fashion Workers Act has a fundamental flaw: It accepts the basic premise—on which the argument rests—that model management companies do not function primarily as booking agents, and that they fall within the "incidental exception." In other words, the Act misses the fact that in reality most model management companies do function primarily as booking agents—even if they claim to function mainly as advisers—and they should be subject to the agency laws of New York instead of having their own set of regulations.

When we ignore or do not understand how the modeling industry functions, we cannot create sufficiently applicable laws; i.e., when we create laws to regulate model management companies that are based on the idea that the incidental exception applies, we are creating laws that do not acknowledge the realities of the modeling industry, and it allows model management companies that function as unlicensed agents to continue to do so. With the Fashion Workers Act, modeling agencies that claim to be management companies have a get-out-of-jail-free card. The law is conforming based on how these companies hold themselves out—i.e., based on the claim that they are not agencies—rather than requiring these companies to conform to laws that reflect reality. There are certainly parts of the Act that will benefit models, but the biggest issue will go unaddressed.

Models who support the Fashion Workers Act cannot be expected to analyze New York law in the same way that a lawyer could to make sure that the Act is effective, and policymakers cannot be expected to understand the inner workings of the modeling industry in the same way that a model could. This is the knowledge gap. And such a gap could result in more and more regulation that has little effect. The existing law is clear—it just needs to be enforced.

**

Just because something is the norm does not make it right.

The confusion over the agent-manager distinction is particularly prevalent in states like New York, where there is no specific model or talent agency Act, but rather several separate laws that need to be read together to understand how they would apply to modeling. Due to the lack of clarity, some model managers do not know that procuring work for their models as a primary function without a license might be construed as improper. They follow the industry norm that has been solidified over years by bigger agencies, and assume that it is the right way to conduct business. They often model their contracts after bigger agency contracts, and tell prospective models that their contract is standard in the industry.

Some other managers are aware of these laws and still decide to operate as agents without a license, knowing that they may be taking a legal risk in doing so but also knowing that they have some practical protection due to the fact that most of the applicable laws that they are flouting are not understood or enforced. These managers will hand models a contract, often confidently declaring that it is a good contract and that any entertainment lawyer would confirm that it is a standard contract in the modeling industry.

Some managers go as far as to tell models that they don't need to spend money to have a lawyer look over the contract, or they will tell models that the contract is not negotiable, or they will indirectly pressure models to sign without giving them time to even read the contract themselves.

It can be difficult for anyone—model or otherwise—to discern when something that is widely accepted is morally impermissible. Most models sign representation contracts without reading them. They do this mainly for two reasons: 1) they think that it is too expensive to hire a lawyer to review the contract, and 2) they think that their agency has their best interests at heart and thus the contract must be fine to sign. Another reason that models sign representation contracts without reading them is that they either feel intimidated by their agents or are blinded by the shine of the opportunity. Often models are called into the agency for an in-person meeting and are offered a contract during the meeting. The agent will hand the model a pen and tell the model that they can get everything set up in their system right away—as soon as the contract is signed—and they are so excited to start working together. In this situation, some models lack the confidence to say that they would like a few days to read over the contract, or they are so grateful to finally have an agency show interest in them that they happily sign on the spot.

Some models will indeed bring their contract to a lawyer—usually an entertainment lawyer, because that seems to make the most sense. However, not all entertainment lawyers understand the modeling industry. As we have seen, the talent agency laws in states like New York have forced modeling agencies to write their contracts in a peculiar way such that there is no indication on paper that they are operating questionably in any way. Fashion is often seen as a branch of entertainment law, but unless an entertainment lawyer has extensive knowledge of the modeling industry specifically, he too might be fooled by modeling contracts. Even fashion lawyers don't often have specific knowledge about modeling contracts because they often focus mainly on representing brands.

Without industry knowledge, a model representation contract may look like a standard talent management contract. It may even state that it is a "personal management" contract rather than a model management contract—a term more commonly used in the film, television, and music industries to refer to a talent manager who represents actors, actresses, musicians, and singers.

One example of how this might be problematic: If you bring your modeling contract to an entertainment lawyer who doesn't understand the industry, he might think that the client service fee clause, which states that the agency charges the client a fee in addition to taking a commission from the model's earnings, is "double-dipping" and try to remove it. This happens more frequently with entertainment lawyers than fashion lawyers, but some fashion lawyers who focus only on the brand side of fashion get confused by this clause as well. If you bring this issue to your potential agent, they will likely decide that you are difficult and are trying to regulate things between the agency and the client that you have no business regulating, and it might become harder to negotiate the rest of your contract.

The problem with a model management contract is not necessarily that it might not be standard, but that a standard modeling contract can be oppressive. Just because it is the norm does not make it right—legally or morally.

Some contracts will state that if a manager "in [their] sole discretion" advances payment for any model expenses, they can recoup that money by deducting from the model's paycheck. They usually don't define "model expenses," they aren't required to provide the model with receipts, and they don't say anything about a maximum amount they will advance. This means that you as a model could be working regularly but seeing every penny earned going to the manager to cover these mysterious model expenses that may, in reality, more accurately be classified as company expenses. You should have control over how your manager spends your money; any model expenses should be approved by you in writing in advance.

Because models—especially early-stage models—usually have no leverage, they can wind up signing a representation contract and then become stuck in a cycle of debt to their agency where they cannot leave the agency until they have repaid their debts, but they get deeper into debt the longer they are with the agency. Why does the agency keep them on their roster? They still earn a 20% or more commission on jobs the model works, plus usually they charge the client a 20% service fee on top of that, so even if they are spending money on behalf of the model and the model is in the red, the agency is making money.

Another example: A modeling contract may include a clause that states that if the manager has not been paid by a client within a certain period of time after the model has completed an assignment, the model will be responsible for immediately reimbursing the manager for any sum of money advanced to the model in connection with the assignment. This means that if a client doesn't pay, the manager is not obligated to chase down the payment. The model winds up not getting paid for a job that would have covered the sums advanced, meaning the model ends up paying the manager without the model getting paid.

Another variation of this clause states that the manager has the right to chase down money owed by a client at the model's expense—again with no limit on how much will be charged to the model. This means that if the manager hires a lawyer to recover money owed, it is the model who will be responsible for the lawyer's fees. Given that the manager already takes 20% of the model's gross income, this could again leave the model in the red while the manager makes money.

Not every agency is like this, but from a model's perspective, enough agencies will have clauses like these in their contracts that it seems normal. This is not normal. If these contracts were taken out of the context of the modeling industry and read in the context of any other industry, they would never be signed. But models have little leverage to negotiate; it is very easy for agencies to walk away from a representation offer and move on to another "less difficult" model.

Often the reason that model managers claim that a contract is not negotiable is that they don't know what the contract says, and they either don't want to go back to their company's lawyer or their agency doesn't have a lawyer and their contract is simply copied from another agency contract that they have seen.

When you as a model have a lawyer review your modeling contract, as you should, you will usually have questions and comments to send back to the manager before signing. Sometimes, it is clear that your manager has no clue what the contract actually means, because the responses that you are given make no sense. Your manager might tell you that a term means one thing, but if that is not what it specifically says in the contract, your manager's interpretation of the term is meaningless. They don't understand the contract, they tell you terms mean things they don't mean, and they don't want to change the contract to make the term actually mean what they think it means because they don't know how.

To compound this, the modeling industry is often comprised of very young, very inexperienced models from foreign countries who do not easily speak or read the language in which the contract is written. They sign whatever contract is offered to them without reading it because they see it as an opportunity, or sometimes as a way out of a bad situation back home. The industry sees them as very easy prey, and without a union or anyone to turn to for help, they become trapped in a bad contract and find themselves deeper and deeper in debt.

You might wonder at this point why there is no union for models in the same way that there is a union (technically, SAG is a "guild") for actors. Models are generally considered to be independent contractors, not employees, so they cannot join a union. However, this is another area in which the existing laws fail to be enforced to the detriment of models. Based on the factors that distinguish an independent contractor from an employee, models would more accurately be described as employees. That is, in the United States, there is a legal definition of "independent contractor." Because this definition exists, it does not matter whether a contract states that someone is an independent contractor. It is not possible to contract out of the law—meaning even if both parties agree to something, if existing law says otherwise, then the parties' agreement means nothing. They both still need to follow the codified law, even if they agreed otherwise in their contract. This means that if your modeling contract says that you are an independent contractor but you fit the legal definition of an employee, then you are an employee.

What defines an employee? For example, a court would look at how much control the client—in modeling, this would often be the brand hiring the model—has over the model. To determine "control," the court would look at whether the client tells the model what time to show up to a shoot, how they should look when they arrive (freshly manicured?), and similar. Generally the answers to the relevant questions determining "control" point to the model being an employee.

Here again, though, no one is looking too closely at this. Some individual cases have been brought before judges who have found based on factors like the ones delineated above that the models were indeed employees. But most models don't bring lawsuits to make this determination, and the models that do bring lawsuits don't get widespread attention. Even if a model were to argue her status as an independent contractor at the contract stage instead of at the lawsuit stage, she would likely be seen as difficult and her offer would be rescinded (or, more likely, she would be "ghosted" by the agency), or clients would refuse to work with her because it is easier for them to classify her as an independent contractor.

Many of the issues that persist in the modeling industry continue to be issues because models fear retaliation. If a model complains about her agency, or negotiates too hard, she might be labeled "difficult" or risk her agency not sending her out for work. Because of the way modeling contracts are structured, models have few defenses for retaliation.

We wouldn't necessarily need models to be classified as employees so that they could join a union if they were just treated fairly. The unfortunate reality is that it has become accepted to treat models poorly, and many models accept poor treatment because they believe that it is just part of being a model.

This should not be the reality, and you do not need to accept poor treatment as a model. Not all agents are unfair or malicious, and you need to find one that will treat you properly both as a human and as a professional model.

***

Three different terms are commonly used to refer to model agents, but each has its own definition.

Model agent, model manager, and personal manager are three terms that you might see in a model representation agreement. "Agent" will only appear in the contract if the agency is actually licensed, even though it most accurately reflects what "model managers" and "personal managers" do for models.

The difference between an agent and a manager can be thought of as follows: Agents book models work and are legally permitted to negotiate their contracts, and are usually motivated by earning as much money as possible as soon as possible. Managers, by contrast, help models make decisions that are best for their long-term career goals, and are motivated by potential greater future earnings as a model's star power increases. Managers will tell their models if an agent is the right fit for them, or if a certain job will help or hinder their career. Managers are not permitted to negotiate contracts. It is a difference in motivation, career strategy, and timeframe that leads to a difference in the actual work of agents versus managers.

The distinction is clearer in the film and television industry. Many actors will first sign with a manager who will work to develop the actor's career. Part of that development often includes introducing the actor to an appropriate agent. While some

Hollywood managers also inappropriately function primarily as booking agents, it does not happen to the degree that it happens in the modeling industry. In general, the biggest talent agencies are not purporting to be management companies, while the biggest modeling agencies are.

In both entertainment and fashion, talent and models might receive one of two different types of management contracts. In entertainment, actors might be offered a "talent management" or a "personal management" contract. In fashion, models might be offered a "model management" or "personal management" contract. A talent management contract will generally specify that the primary purpose of the manager is to manage the actor's career in film and television, and often related areas like commercials or theater. A model management contract generally specifies that the manager will manage the model's modeling career, and will specify many types of modeling, including commercials.

Sometimes, talent management contracts and model management contracts specify a larger scope—that is, they include other fields of management such as publishing. However, when the scope is more broad, the contract will generally not be deemed a "talent" or "model" management contract, but a personal management contract. Personal management contracts do not limit the scope of the manager's representation to one field or industry.

If you are a model and sign a personal management contract, it might give your manager the exclusive right to manage your career in modeling, film, television, publishing, music, social media, advertising, licensing, branding, etc. These types of contracts are generally reserved for managers that actually intend to turn their client into a global brand. For example, if you are a model and envision a career for yourself that includes not only modeling but perhaps also launching a clothing or cosmetics line, acting in films, recording an album, starting a production company, or building your brand in any way beyond the modeling industry, you would benefit from having a good personal manager.

If you sign a personal management contract with your modeling agency, they may specify that they exclusively control each of these areas, but will more than likely only try to book you for modeling jobs. If you are at a point in your career where the agency really does pursue these other opportunities for you, you were likely not presented with the standard modeling contract that is offered to new or unknown models—you were likely able to negotiate a more tailored contract with your agency.

The danger with entering into a personal management contract when you intend to enter into a model management contract is that it is all-encompassing. Your manager will earn a 20% commission not only on your modeling income, but on income from your other endeavors as well.

Many models who sign with modeling agencies have or plan to start income-producing side businesses that are tangentially related to modeling or to the fashion or entertainment industries. For example, a model might host a podcast and earn money from advertisers. Unless this source of income is excluded from the contract, it is not considered independent and outside the scope of the personal management contract, and the manager will take a 20% cut from the model's podcast advertisement earnings, even though what the manager does in reality is limited to booking modeling jobs.

If you are offered a modeling contract and have either existing unrelated business ventures or future plans to start one in which your model manager is not involved, these ventures must explicitly be carved out of your representation contract. As a model, you must also explain to your manager why this needs to be clarified in writing so that it does not seem like you are simply trying to withhold commissions that would rightfully be owed.

Most modeling agents who focus on booking you modeling jobs for short-term income and don't intend to make you a star (or expect you to become one) have no problem excluding these other business ventures. Most money comes from commercial modeling, and most models who become celebrities are not commercial models. Your agent will likely be comfortable earning commissions from your largely anonymous commercial work.

But some agents do have a problem excluding these other business ventures from your contract. Your agent—who purports to be a personal manager—might argue that she has helped to raise your profile by booking you modeling jobs, and if she were not your manager your podcast wouldn't have as many listeners and thus you would not have as many advertising dollars, so she is entitled to 20%. This would only be true in limited circumstances, again, because of the nature of commercial modeling and what it takes to start to build a name for yourself as a model. In general, a model agent who focuses on booking you modeling jobs does not substantially contribute to the advancement of your career in the same way that a true personal manager would. And this is why it is important that your modeling contract conform to the reality of your relationship with your agent—which is, as we have seen, exceptionally difficult given the dishonest use of the term "manager" by unlicensed agents.

An agency contract is much more commonly found in the entertainment world, or in California modeling agencies. Talent agency contracts in general are more fair, and union actors have the added benefit of union protections, though not all actors are immediately able to join a union. Talent and model agency contracts are offered by licensed agents in the entertainment and modeling world. These contracts will explicitly state that the agent will endeavor to procure work for the actor/model. Sometimes they include the right but not the obligation to guide their client in making career decisions. This means that the agency will write that they "may" advise and counsel, but not that they "must." It is clear in these contracts that their primary purpose is to book work for their client. Whereas in New York licensed agents are limited to collecting a 10% commission, California law does not dictate a commission cap. The entertainment industry standard commission has evolved to be 10%

due to union regulations, but licensed modeling agents in California generally still take 20% for most non-union bookings as they do in New York.

While agency contracts as a whole may be more fair than modeling contracts, licensed modeling agencies in California offer contracts that are still heavily influenced by their New York counterparts, and some of their terms remain undesirable. Because of the regulations in California, these contracts are nearly impossible to negotiate. The California Labor Commissioner requires that talent agencies submit their contracts for approval. Once approved, if any substantial changes are made, the contract must be submitted again to the Labor Commissioner for approval. Minor changes do not need to be approved, but minor issues that require minor changes are not going to be dealbreakers for models; these are not the most important changes.

When modeling contracts contain clauses that could get the model into debt with her agency in New York, those clauses can usually be negotiated—even if the agency says that they are non-negotiable. In California, while those clauses may still exist in the contract, the agency is likely to be unwilling to go through the approval process again with the Labor Commissioner to sign one model. If more models would refuse to sign the contract containing those clauses, then the agency might be incentivized to make the change. But because most models don't read their contracts and don't want to lose an opportunity to sign with an agency, agents in California can more easily say that the contract is non-negotiable, and if the model doesn't like a term then she does not need to sign. How quickly agents will tell models, "Best of luck in your future endeavors!" is an indication of how replaceable models are to agents—and that viewpoint does not change once a model is signed.

When you are offered a model representation contract you must look at the moral implications as well as the legal implications.

Not every undesirable clause is an indication of immorality. The drafters of any contract will almost always write the contract in their own favor, and it is up to the other party to try to make the contract more fair. Sometimes certain clauses that seem one-sided are just the result of the agency making a business decision. They may be unfavorable, but they are not clearly taking advantage of the other party.

But sometimes it is a bit more than just a business decision, and the agency is indeed clearly trying to take advantage of the other party because they rely on the likelihood that on the other side of the negotiating table is an eager model who will not read the contract.

You may be inclined to sign whatever you have been given because it is an opportunity. But because the modeling industry is largely unregulated, while certain things may not be illegal, they may be immoral—and they should be illegal, and probably will be in the future. Until then, if you are presented with a questionable contract, you need to consider whether you want to go into business with someone— potentially long-term—who would take certain underhanded actions just because he or she can.

No one will protect your career like you will, and one thing that could potentially stall or damage that career is teaming up with people who have loose morals. Be discerning from the outset to position yourself for success.

***

Your model and talent management contracts may be in conflict.

While the difference between a personal management contract, a talent or model management contract, and an agency contract may be clear in theory, in practice the terms are used loosely and sometimes considered interchangeable. Legally this can lead to conflicting contracts, and practically this can lead to you not being able to work with someone that you should have on your team. That is, if you are pursuing both acting and modeling and you have a manager for each, your contracts with both might be incompatible.

While many management contracts state that your manager is an exclusive, personal manager focused on the development of your career, in reality, most managers—especially in the early stages of your career—are not general personal managers, but work specifically to develop your career in either the modeling industry or the entertainment industry. This is because their expertise generally lies in one industry or the other. A talent manager, for example, will have film and television agency contacts, insight into the best acting classes, and knowledge of upcoming productions. A model manager will know when fashion week casting occurs, who the upcoming designers are, and will have relationships with fashion brands. If you work in both industries, even though they overlap in many instances, you want to be able to work with a manager who will focus on entertainment as well as a manager who will focus on modeling.

However, the exclusivity requirement in a contract that purports to be a "personal management" contract technically means that you are only permitted to work with one manager, regardless of type. If you have multiple career trajectories and are offered a management contract by someone who is not in reality capable of functioning as a general personal manager, you must ensure that the contract specifies the industry or type of work that your manager is expected to manage. Your model management contract should say model management. Your talent management contract should say talent management. This way you will be free to work with other managers who specialize in different industries. That is, even if your modeling contract says that your model manager also controls your work in film and TV, you most likely, realistically, still need a talent manager to handle your work in entertainment.

The exclusivity clause will generally go on to detail that the "personal manager" controls the model's work in anything tangentially related to media, fashion, or entertainment such as film/TV, music, and publishing, and that the model is not permitted to sign with another agent or manager in any space without the manager's prior approval.

Again, the reality is that most modeling agencies focus on modeling, not personal management, which means that if there is a chance that now or in the future you might want to branch out into something other than modeling, you need to be free to work with booking agents in film/TV, music managers, etc. And even if you think that you only want to model, you should still be free to work with other agents and managers in different industries. If your modeling agent is really only going to focus on booking you modeling jobs—which is most likely the case—then you should limit your contract to just modeling. You may change your mind about what you want to pursue in the future, and even if you don't, there is no harm in being free to choose.

***

Keep track of your own finances even if your modeling agency says that they will do it for you.

One of the most pervasive issues in the modeling industry is a lack of financial awareness among models. Many models rely on their agents to keep track of their finances. They assume that when a client pays the agency, the agency will pay the model the full amount due minus the agency's 20% commission. It is not that simple. Often models find themselves earning nothing from their work, or even in debt to their agency despite having worked several jobs, and they don't understand why. There are several reasons for this, and there are simple ways to avoid this issue. It starts with understanding modeling contracts and extends to understanding how the industry functions, because not everything is captured by the contract.

Sometimes an agency contract will state that the agency will keep a "reserve account" for the model. Even if the agency claims that model expenses will be kept to a minimum, they will retain thousands of dollars in the reserve account and replenish it before paying the model for jobs she has completed. The money in the reserve account is not agency money, however, it is the model's money.

This means that if your contract says that the agency will keep $5,000.00 in your reserve account, and the agency advances you $1,500.00 for a job that pays $2,500.00—let's say to buy a plane ticket—they will deduct $1,500.00 from the $2,500.00 that the job paid in order to bring your reserve account back up to $5,000.00. There are two things to remember here: While an agency may call this "advancing" money, it is in fact your money to begin with in the reserve account. If the agency needs to buy a plane ticket for you, it will come out of the reserve account—not out of the agency's pocket. Second, not only will the agency deduct from your $2,500.00 paycheck to replenish your reserve account, but they will also deduct their commission. A 20% commission will take $500.00 immediately out of the $2,500.00 job rate. If the agency also moves $1,500.00 into your reserve account, you are left with a $500.00 paycheck for a $2,500.00 job, assuming that you had zero additional expenses—no manicures, no coffees, no taxis, no taxes.

At this point, many models will be confused. Doesn't the agency pay for a model's work-related expenses?

When agents offer a model a contract, they often talk about how the agency will pay for a model's transportation, hotels, meals, etc. A lot of models mistakenly believe that this means that they are about to be treated to an all-expenses-paid life of luxury, because the agent will neglect to tell the model that any money the agency spends on the model will need to be repaid by the model. The agency does not pay for a model's work-related expenses. It is a common misconception that they do. They usually write this in a management contract as well, but it is sometimes written in a way that makes models think that the agency is only talking about minor expenses. That is, the contract will focus on things like printing and mailing, but not larger expenses like plane tickets.

For example, if your first paycheck nets you $1,000.00 but your agency advanced $1,500.00, the amount that you take home is $0. This will happen until the agency is fully paid back. An easy way to get into debt with your agency is by not tracking what comes in and what goes out. And if your contract is terminated for some reason by the agency, anything you owe the agency will become due immediately, so you cannot rely on future jobs to pay them back slowly. Keep track of everything and pay for what you can yourself so that you don't wind up in debt to your agency.

An agent might tell a model that the agency tries to keep expenses to a minimum, and the contract might say that they will "try" to tell the model beforehand when they are going to spend her money. First, if expenses are kept to a minimum, why keep thousands of dollars in a reserve account? Second, stating that the agency will "try" to do something has no actual effect. When they use this language, they are not required to tell a model when they are about to spend her money—they do it without her knowing, and she likely first becomes aware that her money was spent when she receives a statement from her agency—if they indeed send her a statement (sometimes agencies require that a model ask for a statement instead of sending one automatically to their models regularly).

If an agency attaches a list of possible expenses and their estimated costs, it is important to remember that the list is non-exhaustive, meaning that if the agency lists as possible expenses comp cards, website fees, and shipping costs, it does not preclude them from spending your money on other expenses not listed. Usually when an agency attaches this list of minor expenses they will include an estimated price for each. Some agencies include accurate prices, but many agencies heavily overestimate the cost of these supposedly minimal expenses.

Overblown estimates for minor expenses are a red flag—it should tell you as a model that the way the agency makes money is not necessarily by finding you work, but through dishonest accounting. If an agency charges you $100.00 per month for comp card printing but you never see those comp cards being used, you need to review this expense with your agency. If you are charged $300.00 for shipping, you need to know what the agency shipped on your behalf. Oftentimes, if a model had paid for these expenses herself, she would have been charged a fraction of what the agency charged her.

The issue here is that while an agency can demand receipts from a model, it will be more difficult in practice for a model to obtain receipts from an agency. When there is a question about an expense, often models will either not hear back from their agency when they try to open a conversation, or the agency will send them a statement that contains numbers self-reported by the agency, but no receipts.

To avoid being overcharged, not only should a model pay for her own expenses and keep track of her own finances, but she should have a clause in her contract that states that she must give prior approval in writing for any advances or expenses that the agency will pursue on her behalf. Generally, as we saw earlier, the opposite of this is what is stated in the contract—agencies will write that they can, in their "sole discretion," advance payment to the model for any expenses they deem necessary. They do not need her approval, and they do not need to tell her that they are spending her money.

Your modeling agency should not have the freedom to spend your money without you knowing about it. This is not only because you can find yourself in debt to your agency, as previously illustrated, but because you should always, in general, be in control of your own finances. Trying to control your money is an overreach by the agency.

They sometimes say that they include this clause for the sake of efficiency, but this is a weak argument. If your agency urgently needs additional comp cards for you, they can tell you to print new comp cards for them by a certain date. Then, if you tell them that you are unable to do so, you can give them approval to print them on your behalf. This exchange does not take long—and if the agency needs comp cards so urgently that they don't have time to ask you to print them, you should ask your agency why they left replenishing your stack of comp cards to the last minute. They may have a valid reason, but more than likely you will find that their urgent need is not so urgent.

As a general rule, in order to stay in control of your finances and to be aware of how much you are earning, do not accept advances from your agency, and pay for your own expenses yourself. If you do this, your agency will not need to keep a model reserve account, and any money that you earn from your work will go directly to you instead of being held in a "just in case" fund by your agency.

Some models are fine with limiting a reserve account to $500.00 for minor expenses. This is not unreasonable if you would prefer that your agency handle minor expenses, if you keep track of what they spend on your behalf, and if what they charge you is in line with what you would be charged if you paid out of pocket.

When reserve accounts maintain sums in the thousands, it is an indication that the agency views the account not only as a source of money to pay for associated modeling expenses, but as a way to hold money in case they bring a legal claim against you that could potentially result in a money judgment in their favor, meaning that you are directed to pay the agency a certain sum.

Given that many disputes between models and their agencies are financial in nature, eliminating the object of the potential dispute is a good way to avoid the dispute. That is, if there is no reserve account and a model is in charge of her own money and expenses, the agency's accounting responsibilities are minimal, and there is less possibility that they will find any reason to say that a model owes them money. Sometimes the best way to avoid issues is not to "contract them away," but to simplify the working relationship such that those issues naturally do not arise.

While agents might try to maintain a reserve account in case a model owes them money, the more common scenario is that the agency will owe the model money.

Accounting errors happen, but they are less likely to become a real issue if models check the work of their agency. We have seen that agents will often advance money to models and then recover that money by taking it from the model's future pay. Sometimes months will pass and a model will realize that she is in major debt to her agency and cannot figure out why. There are sometimes duplicate hotel charges, instances in which an agency inadvertently charged plane tickets to the wrong model's account, random unidentified expenses that the agency can't or won't explain—these are all common—and avoidable—issues.

The way that you can avoid these issues as a model is to keep every receipt associated with a job that you have booked, and make a spreadsheet for yourself with columns: This is the job, this is what it paid, these are the associated expenses, this is the final amount that I should have received, and this is what I actually received from my agency. If those last two columns don't match, ask your agency why you received X amount when you should have gotten Y. Do this immediately, not in six months, when everything is going to be more difficult to trace.

This does not necessarily need to be a confrontation, but a conversation. Sometimes the agency will have made a mistake and will correct the error, and sometimes the model miscalculated something that the agency needs to point out to her. But sometimes it does indeed turn into an adversarial situation—particularly if the agency cannot or does not want to explain the discrepancy.

Whether financial in nature or not, if you go to your agency with an issue that requires their assistance to resolve and are met with resistance or dismissiveness, this is a good indication that your working relationship with your agency is no longer working.

Another potential accounting error is a client service fee being charged to your account. A client service fee should never directly or indirectly come out of your pocket. There is usually a term in modeling contracts that says that your management company will not only take 20% of your gross income, but will charge the client who books you an additional 20% "service fee." This "double-dipping" is standard industry practice. It means that your manager will take 20% of your gross income, plus charge the client another 20% fee on top of the job rate offered to you. This is also how your agent makes a decent amount of money off of you even if you do not work frequently.

Another way this can be written is that a 33% fee will be "divided over the client and the model." This takes the place of the client service fee language and the agency commission language, and is confusing to many models but it means essentially the same thing.

For example, with standard commission contract language, if you book a job that pays $1,000.00, the agency will take $200.00 from your paycheck (their 20% commission) and pay you $800.00, assuming that there are no associated expenses. Separately, the agency would charge the client another $200.00 as a 20% service fee. The result is that the client is ultimately charged $1,200.00, you receive $800.00, and your agency receives $400.00. The client generally factors in the agency service fee, and the breakdown might say that the job pays "$1,000.00+20%." This 20% does not go to you, but to your agency.

With the language stating that the 33% fee will be divided over the client and the model, the billing process can be illustrated by analyzing the payment steps in a different order. For the same job, the agency will bill the client $1,200.00 total. From this, the agency removes the 20% service fee of $200.00. But 20% of $1,200.00 is not $200.00! Correct—recall that the client service fee should never come out of the model's pocket. So, the service fee must be calculated based on the model's job rate and taken before the agency takes its commission from the total earned by the model. If the job rate is $1,000.00, even if the client is charged $1,200.00, it is only the $1,000.00 that is earned by the model that is subject to the agency's 20% commission.

So, after having removed the first $200.00, the agency is left with $1,000.00, from which they then deduct their 20% commission of $200.00. In total, the agency earns $400.00, which is 33% of the full $1,200.00 invoice. You will see that this 33% was indeed split evenly between the model and the client, each of whom paid the agency $200.00 in commissions and fees.

When the job pays a sum other than $1,000.00 and the contract uses this 33% language, the numbers are less straightforward and it is easy for a model to become confused when reviewing statements from her agency. When you are reviewing your statements, remember that this 33% language functions the same way as the 20%+20% language; you must know the full amount that is due to you specifically before the agency takes its commission—the client service fee will never be due to you, so this should not be a factor in your calculations. Then you can make sure that the agency's numbers are correct, and that they are not taking more commission from your paycheck than they should.

However, because your goal is to be a model and not an administrative assistant or an accountant, a better approach would be to have a conversation with your agency if you see this 33% language in your contract. Ask the agency if they can use the standard 20%+20% language for clarity. It may even make their own accounting more straightforward. Again, sometimes agents will be unwilling or unable to change the contract—sometimes because they don't understand what the contract says—but you should always ask. If you present it as being beneficial to them as well, they may make more of an effort to understand what you are asking.

It is critical that the "service fee" clause be read and understood in conjunction with other contract terms with which it may interact so that you do not wind up being partly responsible for collecting an unpaid service fee, or docked pay due to its non-payment based on other seemingly unrelated contract terms. Read your contract as a whole, not just as individual parts, so that you don't wind up owing money after a modeling job.

More specifically, recall that your modeling agreement may include a clause that states that if your manager has not been paid by a client within a certain period of time after you have completed an assignment, you will be responsible for immediately reimbursing your manager for any sum of money advanced to you in connection with the assignment.

This means that if a client doesn't pay, your manager is not obligated to chase down the payment. You wind up not getting paid for a job that would have covered the sums advanced, meaning that you end up paying your manager without getting paid yourself. Your manager breaks even and you are in the red. Be careful with advances, and with terms that allow your manager to walk away from collecting money owed— at your expense.

There is an even more dire situation that models can find themselves in due to a client not paying, and this is one of a few terms that should be considered a dealbreaker. Some modeling contracts will state that if a client doesn't pay the agent within a certain amount of time, the agency may—in its sole discretion—pursue collection options. These collection efforts might include working with a debt collector or a lawyer to recover the money owed to the agency. The issue is that most contracts state that the costs associated with this debt collection, including legal fees, are to be divided equally between the agency and the model, or more commonly, borne entirely by the model. Recall that because the contract says "in its sole discretion," the agency will be able to pursue debt collection without your consent. This means that the agency can run up legal costs that you cannot afford, and you cannot tell them to stop. Recall also that the agency makes money even when you don't. You might net $0 from a job due to expenses and paying the agency's commission, but the agency still earns money both from the commission it takes from your gross pay and from the client service fee. In some instances, the agency is more incentivized to collect from a non-paying client than you are. And if you are the sole individual paying for the collection, the agency has every reason to pursue a client for non-payment on your dime.

Sometimes the contract will say that the agency can, in its sole discretion, pursue collections, but it doesn't specify who pays. Usually when models question this part of the contract the agency will say that it's not important, there's a very low risk of this happening, they've never had to do this before, and they don't work with clients who don't pay.

It may be true that there is a low risk of it happening, but that doesn't mean that there is no risk. If there were no risk, they wouldn't require that it remain in the contract. And if it does happen, the consequences can be dire for a model who cannot afford to pursue collections.

You don't usually contract for when things go right, but for when things go wrong. Many parts of a contract might seem like they are overkill—like the risk of them happening is so low that there is no reason for them to even be in the contract. Including clauses about what to do if a pandemic were to become an issue, for example, seems like a far-out idea until it actually happens. And when it does happen, you want to be able to look to your contract to tell you how to handle the situation.

It is true that when you enter into an agreement with someone, you generally don't expect things to go downhill; if you did, you probably wouldn't sign the contract. When things are going well, there is little need to look back on the contract terms. It is when someone does something that they are not supposed to—or does not do something that they are supposed to—that contracts become useful. This is when you can point to specific terms to get everyone back on track.

And this is why it is better to have contracts reviewed before you sign them. You can hope and expect that things will go right, but you should be prepared for them to go wrong. That way, if something does happen, you have an airtight contract in place to protect you.

Again, part of what makes modeling contracts particularly dangerous is that they usually do not reflect the reality of the agent-model relationship, and this, as we've seen, is because of the way the industry has evolved around certain laws. This means that if something goes wrong—and in the modeling industry, something going wrong is a very real possibility—it is going to be very difficult for you as a model to get yourself out of a bad situation. If you have your contracts reviewed by a lawyer before you sign them, you are more likely to be protected against things like being wholly responsible for the costs of the agency's decision to pursue debt collection.

One final note about model management contracts not always being what they seem: You might think that you should be able to understand what your modeling contract is saying because it is written in plain, simple English. But in a legal context, especially in the context of contracts and how the words are put together within the contract, the words may take on a different meaning. The reason lawyers can spend so much time going back and forth on contracts is because of these kinds of sneaky linguistic acrobatics that might be invisible at first glance.

The danger here is that some lawyers get so into the weeds of possible interpretations and interactions and outcomes that the deal winds up falling apart. If you want the deal to go through—meaning, if you ultimately want to sign with a modeling agency—you need to find the point at which you are the most protected that you can possibly be without causing the agency to walk away. But this should not come at the cost of you accepting dealbreakers like being responsible for paying legal fees and expenses associated with debt collection if the agency unilaterally decides to pursue a non-paying client.

While you and your lawyer might be able to negotiate a contract, sometimes there are contracts that you just should not sign, and the deal should not go through. There are some red flags that may be apparent not due to the specific words of the contract terms as read individually, but what they mean together, as a whole, and what they tell you about going into business with the individual or entity on the other side of the table, as previously discussed.

This is not something that you should try to figure out on your own though, and it is not necessarily something that a lawyer focused on a different area of law—such as entertainment law, as we saw earlier—would be able to help you with. This is normal—lawyers don't practice in every area of law.

But it is why you need to contact a lawyer who speaks the language of contracts and also speaks the language of the modeling industry before you sign any modeling contracts.

Sometimes agents will push back when a model questions a term in the contract. If she says that she wants prior approval in writing before an agency can spend money on her behalf instead of giving the agency "sole discretion" to do so, an agent might come back and say that they would of course prefer that a model pay for her own expenses and would only advance money if the model requests.

This may be a comforting communication, but it is not what the contract says. Even if the model has this statement in writing, the contract likely says that communications outside of the contract hold no legal weight. Whatever the agent may tell the model that he does not subsequently include in the contract means nothing, legally. However, because sometimes agents don't understand their own contract, they don't realize this, and if a model pushes to have the agent adjust the contract to reflect what the agent thinks the contract says, the agent might decide that working with the model is not worth the trouble.

Negotiating modeling contracts is unlike negotiating any other type of contract. Agents are very quick to walk away, and industry norms have a strong hold on contracts. Models have very little leverage. When models question the most dangerous terms in modeling contracts—such as being responsible for unlimited collection costs—agents usually dismiss their concerns by saying that it has never happened before so there is no need to worry about it.

Even if there is a slim chance of it happening, it is not a 0% chance. If there were no chance of it happening, it would not need to be included in the contract. It may be unlikely to come to pass, but if it does, the model could be in severe trouble. However, the alternative for most models is to not sign the contract.

So, for the most part, negotiating modeling contracts is less about negotiating than it is about assessing risk. Are you as a model willing to run the risk of getting into huge amounts of debt due to collection costs—even if unlikely—in order to have a chance at getting modeling work through this agency?

This is also why it is important to work with a lawyer who understands the modeling industry; the negotiation strategy will be different, as will the conversation about risks that you are willing to take in order for the deal to go through.

***

Your agent's lawyer works for your agent, not for you.

We have discussed model and talent management contracts, personal management contracts, and agency contracts. There is a fourth type of contract that you might come across as a model, and it is an amalgamation of all the confusion that you might encounter in all other types of contracts. This is the mother agency contract.

First, what is a mother agent? There is a technical definition and a practical definition, and as with other terminology in the modeling industry, the reality does not match the language.

Technically, the purpose of a mother agent is to place models with booking agents in various markets. Recall that booking agents in the modeling industry often refer to themselves as management companies, but their primary purpose is to book work for models. The term "agent" generally triggers questions about licensing, but since mother agents usually do not procure work for the model, they do not need to be licensed.

A mother agency contract will sometimes use the term "agent" but detail model management obligations such as advising on a model's career rather than agency (booking) obligations. So, if you are working with a mother agent and a model manager, your mother agent will act more like a manager and your model manager will act more like an agent.

A model may either sign with a mother agent first, who will then try to get the model signed with a "model management company," or a model can sign directly with a management company without having a mother agent.

If you sign directly with a management company, that company generally automatically becomes your mother agent. If there is a clause in your contract that states this, you need to ask whether the agency will actively try to place you with other agencies in other markets. If you sign with an agency in New York, their territory is often limited to New

York, meaning that their contract will state that you must work exclusively with them in New York but can work with other agencies to book you work in other locations. If your New York agent—who books you work in New York—automatically becomes your mother agent, you usually won't work in other markets unless your New York agency places you with other agencies. While many contracts contain this mother agency clause, it is not unusual for model management companies to claim to be your mother agent while having no intention of placing you with agents in other markets. The clause is there because if you do sign with another agency—whether because they scouted you or because you reached out on your own—your original management company wants to make sure that they earn their mother agency commission.

Generally a mother agent will split the commission earned by the booking agent. For example, if a model has both a mother agent and a modeling agent (booking agent/model manager), the modeling agent will take a 20% commission from the model's gross pay, but will pay half of that commission to the mother agent. So, of the model's gross pay, 10% goes to her modeling agent and 10% goes to her mother agent.

Here is another potential pitfall: The way mother agency clauses are written, it sometimes seems to the model that if she works with both a mother agent and a modeling agent, she will be giving up 30% of her commission—10% to the mother agent and 20% to the modeling agent. This is not the case. If the mother agency clause goes into effect because you have signed with another agency in another market (a "subagency") it does not mean that your original agency gets 10% in addition to the 20% you must pay to your subagency—it means that your subagency must cut a check to your original agency. This comes out of their commission, not your paycheck.

Generally the mother agency and the subagency will have a contract between themselves that you won't see. This contract details the requirements of the subagency to pay part of its commission to the mother agency. Here again, make sure that you track your finances to ensure that your representatives are handling your money properly.

You might wonder whether it is possible for the mother agent and the subagent to make a contract between themselves that says that the subagent collects the full 20% and the mother agent collects an additional 10%—meaning that in total, 30% comes out of your paycheck. As a general rule, it is not possible for two parties to make a contract that imposes restrictions or obligations on an unrelated third party.

If hypothetical Cheryl and Mark are talking about buying a boat together, they cannot create a contract that says they will each pay 33% of the cost of the boat, and that their friend Paul will pay the rest. Paul did not agree to this contract, and Paul is not responsible for any payments. This is the same situation with your mother agent and your modeling agent. As long as the commission structure and percentage are clear in your agreements with both agencies individually—that is, the mother agency language in your contracts should indicate that the mother agent and the subagent are to split the 20% commission amongst themselves—then it doesn't matter what their agreement is, because you are contractually only responsible for giving up the 20% commission, not 30%.

One thing to note here is that if you sign a contract containing the mother agency clause, you need to have a conversation with your agency about what their intentions are in terms of placing you in other markets, and what your limitations are. Some agents will get upset if a model continues to apply to agencies in other markets, even if that agent doesn't make any effort to place the model with other agencies. The easiest way for an agency to retaliate is to stop trying to book work for that model—and recall that because of the way the contract is likely written (i.e., it specifically states that the agent will not procure work for the model), the model cannot go back to the agency to complain that they have stopped getting her work, because the agency will come back and say, "That's not what our contract says that we do." Then the model is stuck in a potentially three-year contract (the industry standard) with an agent who has benched her.

If you do have a mother agent or a booking agent who will act like a mother agent and are offered a contract by a subagent, your mother agent will likely want to review the contract. There are two things to remember here: 1) Many mother agents review contracts without having any legal background and think that it's fine to do so because they have seen countless modeling contracts. Exposure to volume is not a sufficient replacement for legal training. 2) The mother agent is not necessarily reviewing the contract to make sure that it is the best contract for you, but to make sure that it is the best contract for the mother agency.

Even if your agent offers to have the agency's lawyer look over a contract purportedly on your behalf, that lawyer's client is still the agency, not you. If something later goes wrong between you and that agency, or if there is something in the contract that would benefit you but would be detrimental to the agency, that lawyer is not going to protect you, and will probably even change the contract to make that detrimental clause go away, which means removing a term that is favorable to you.

Your agent's lawyer works for your agent, not for you. You need your own lawyer from the beginning who is going to look out for you, even if you are told by your agent, as many models are, that you don't need one; and you do not want to find out that you do after you have already signed a bad contract.

Returning to the idea that the model might be stuck in a three-year contract and kept on the sidelines if she upsets her agency: Three-year contracts are standard in the modeling industry. Modeling contracts, unlike contracts that you might come across in any other industry, usually auto-renew for additional one-year terms, but sometimes they auto-renew for additional three-year terms. Anyone who has read contracts outside of the context of the modeling industry tends to find this auto-renewal clause absurd. When models read it, they are worried that three years is a long time—especially in the modeling industry where youth is so heavily valued and in three years a model might age out of the industry entirely.

What is more concerning, however, is that most models do not realize that their agents will not give them a warning when the initial term—the first three years of the contract—is about to expire. Then they are surprised to discover that their contract has auto-renewed and they are stuck in it for another one, two, or three years even if they do not want to stay with their agency.

Agencies do not send models reminders about their contracts; that is, they do not warn models when a contract is about to renew. When a modeling contract auto-renews, it eliminates the ability of the model to renegotiate the contract, and locks the model into an additional term.

If your contract contains language stating that it auto-renews, it will also contain language about a notice period. This notice period may range from thirty days to six months, but the standard is ninety days. This means that at least ninety days before your contract expires, you need to let your agent know if you do not want to renew your contract.

Generally the contract will say that the notice needs to be in writing, signed, and sent by Certified Mail to the agency's address—but usually agencies will accept notice by email if you ask to put that in the contract. Remember, many modeling contracts—and many contracts in general—use language from old contracts. Sometimes they are not sufficiently updated because no one thinks that terms such as those that dictate how to mail notice are important, but practically, if you do want to terminate your contract, email will make it easier for you to do so. This is not a big "ask" and generally agencies are perfectly willing to add email as an acceptable method of termination notice.

The danger of long notice periods is that if you plan to terminate your contract because your relationship with your agency has gone south, the agency may not send you out for work during the entire notice period. This could be for retaliatory purposes, or it could be because they would prefer to invest their time and energy into models with whom they will have a longer, ongoing relationship. If your contract demands six months' notice for termination, you could be out of work for six months but still under an exclusive contract preventing you from working with another agency during that time.

If you want to terminate a contract early, the notice period does not apply. Usually modeling contracts will allow for an agency to terminate the contract at any time for any reason without providing any advance notice to the model. The model has no such right. Some contracts allow for the model to terminate the contract after four to six months of the agency not having found work for the model, provided that the model was ready, willing, and able to accept available jobs. These clauses generally only appear rarely in licensed agency contracts, where the agency does not have to hide the fact that its main purpose is to procure work for the model (recall that model managers are not permitted to procure work for models as their primary function—allowing a model to get out of a contract because a manager has not procured work for her would be a good indication that the primary purpose of the contract and function of the manager is to procure work for the model).

If you are unhappy and want to leave your agency but your contract does not allow you to terminate your relationship early, you are not out of options. Contracts are great to have as a guide, but just because something is not in your contract does not mean that it is not possible.

Often when models want to break their contracts, they first try to find something in the contract that allows them to do so. In reality, the first thing that you should do is have a conversation with your agency. If the relationship has already soured, the agency might not be as open to a conversation. But if something is not working for you, it may not be working for the agency either, and it is possible that they will agree to let you out of the contract early if you are both feeling lackluster about the working relationship.

If you have had payment issues or other problems with your agency that have created a more adversarial environment, they will likely not be as open to this discussion. That is when you would start looking at the contract to see what your options are.

If a model is worried about being trapped in a three-year contract, why can't she just ask to change it to a one-year contract? She can! But she is highly unlikely to succeed. In some instances, a two-year contract is accepted by an agency, but usually only for somewhat more experienced models.

There is a reason that most model representation contracts start with a three-year term. As previously discussed, when you are offered a modeling contract, it is most likely going to be written as a management contract, not a booking agency contract. The contract will say that your manager will advise you and help to develop your career. If this is actually what they are going to do, it might take time to develop you into a marketable model. If you spend six months getting a portfolio together before your manager says that you are finally ready to be seen for potential work, that is six months of time invested in you without a dime going to your manager. So, when you start working, your manager wants to make sure that you have a good amount of time left on your contract so that they can start earning money as a result of the time they invested in you.

Further, they don't want to develop you into a marketable model only to have you move over to a competing agency a short time later. A booking agent—who will try to start booking you immediately—doesn't necessarily need a three-year contract. But most agents that try to start booking you immediately claim that they are managers, not agents, and hand you a three-year contract. The length of your relationship with your agent or manager should depend on what that person intends to do with you in reality—not what the contract claims they intend to do with you. The reality is that the industry functions heavily on inertia, and because a three-year initial term has become the standard, it is unlikely to change regardless of whether your agent is functioning as a booking agent or a true manager.

This is why it is important to remember that the first representation contract you are offered may not be the best offer. Models who are just starting out are particularly prone to accepting any offer that comes their way. They are so excited to finally have an opportunity—any opportunity—that they accept it without question. The impulse is understandably strong—after years of rejection it is natural to want to take the first opportunity that presents itself, because the alternative is potentially another year of agency submissions and rejection. They are often also worried that if they don't sign the contract immediately, the opportunity will disappear. The result is that not only do they not have a lawyer review the contract, but they do not read it themselves.

This is how so many models find themselves in bad contracts—and sometimes bad situations. Not all agencies are disreputable, but the ones that are will prey on young or inexperienced models, relying on the high probability that these models are desperate. The agent will paint a picture for the model of fame and fortune, telling the model how unique she is, how the agency already has plans for her to go to Paris to work, and how they will buy the plane ticket and hotel room for her (remember—agencies do not cover these costs! At best, a client will cover such costs, but unless that was previously arranged, the model pays for these expenses). When it is written out like this, a model might easily be able to identify red flags. But when faced with these types of situations in person, it can be far more difficult to see the warning signs of a disreputable agency, particularly because the model so desperately wants the opportunity to be real.

Be objective, and be cautious. You do not need to be overly skeptical to the point where you decline good opportunities, however, and this is where it becomes important for models to have someone with whom they can discuss these opportunities and their career as a whole. You may think that this person is your agent or manager. That may be true to a certain degree, but if everyone on your team is working on commission, you may not be receiving objective advice.

Recall that there is supposedly a difference in the motivations behind what booking agents do and what managers do. Booking agents are generally interested in the quantity of jobs, and true managers are generally interested in the quality of jobs. Managers are supposed to help you develop your career in the right direction, and sometimes that means turning down jobs that do not advance your career or are wrong for you in some way. It should be a long-term vision rather than an agent's more immediate goals. But as we have seen, many managers actually take on the role of booking agents and submit you for jobs as well.

Even if they do not submit you for jobs themselves, they may just want you to work because whenever you work, they get paid. And when you don't work, they don't get paid. This means that your manager may be submitting you for or advising you to take jobs that aren't right for you just so that they can earn some money. They need to make money to stay in business.

There are some ways to determine which managers are in it for the right reasons. For example, if a manager has a roster of 100 models, you should question whether that manager has the time to spend effectively managing you and your career. Usually true managers have smaller rosters than agents, because their job extends beyond job submissions and is often more time-intensive for individual clients. Make sure that the person acting as your career adviser is acting objectively and is not solely motivated by commission.

Keeping financial motivations in check is necessary for models as well, not just their managers. When you make moral decisions for financial reasons, the outcome is usually unfavorable. If you work in either the entertainment or the modeling industry as an actor or a model, you will most likely at some point be presented with a very tempting payday with some very unsavory strings attached.

Just as your manager must not advise you to pursue an opportunity solely due to a potential commission, the career decisions that you make for yourself cannot be driven solely by finances. While acting and modeling are businesses and finances are certainly a consideration, in fashion and entertainment in particular, financial gain today might mean the end of your career tomorrow. If you are presented with an opportunity and you say, "I'm going to do this shoot because I need to pay my rent this month, but I hope no one sees this," that could be the shoot that everyone is going to see.

Why is this a problem? So much of your success in the acting and modeling industries is about the careful curation of an image. It takes a very long time to craft your public image and only a second to irretrievably destroy it.

For example, if you are vegan but you become the face of a fur brand, this is inauthentic. If you pose for photos that are more racy than artistic and you want to star in family-friendly TV shows, you may cut yourself out of opportunities that are more in line with your career goals because you might inadvertently start building a name for yourself that is not in line with the image and reputation that you want to establish.

As you are building your personal brand, what matters is going to be how people see you, not what the truth is; what is real to the general public is what they think they know. With every job offer that you are on the fence about, ask yourself: If money were not an issue, would I do this? If the answer is absolutely not, then you need to find a different way to pay your rent that month.

If your manager urges you to pursue opportunities that are not in line with your brand image, you need to have a conversation. It may be the case that your manager knows that an opportunity is not completely in line with your career goals, but that it may lead to other, more on-target opportunities. But if your manager encourages you to take jobs solely for short-term financial reasons, you should reevaluate whether your manager is right for you. It is critical to have the right team around you, to know when a relationship is not working, and to have the confidence to let someone go who is not contributing to the advancement of your career.

There will likely be times when there is someone on your team—an agent, manager, publicist, coach—that you like very much as a person. You enjoy working with them, but there is something that is not making sense in your working relationship. They may not have done anything wrong, but perhaps you have outgrown their capabilities, or they are in some other way not quite right for your career at that moment.

You must recognize when these situations arise, and you must have the confidence to replace that person on your team. This may be a difficult conversation, and it may make that person unhappy, but you need to make the best business decisions for yourself. This does not mean that you should freely walk all over people, but it does mean that you need to make deliberate, well-reasoned, logical decisions about who is right for your team.

This is one reason why some people find it impossible to work with their friends or family. For the same reason, some people find that it is only possible to work with their friends or family. Some people worry that making difficult business decisions will negatively affect their personal relationships if they work with friends or family, and some people believe that those are the only people whom they can truly trust. Whether you decide to keep business relationships and personal relationships separate or decide to mix them, the way to preserve relationships—even when difficult decisions must be made—is to communicate. If you are working with an agent and wonder why you haven't booked anything, talk with them about it. They may be working on something for you behind closed doors that takes a bit longer than usual to confirm. If you are working with a manager and want to pursue a different career strategy than the one already in place, have a conversation about why you think you should change the approach. If you don't say anything, your reps will not know that you have concerns; you will ruminate and your reps will proceed as usual.

On the topic of communication, it is important also to give your reps the space that they need to do their job. If you are overly communicative, your agents and managers will be spending their time talking to you rather than trying to find you opportunities. As with all things, there is a balance. Communicate when necessary (for example, if you need advice on which new digitals showcase you best, or when you have something specific to discuss) and check in with reasonable frequency. Otherwise, let your reps do their job.

One topic you should discuss with your agent or manager before even signing your representation agreement with them is what you are and are not comfortable doing on set. If you have limitations, you should let your agent know in advance so that you don't keep turning down jobs. For example, if you are not comfortable wearing real fur at a photo shoot, tell your agent. Don't wait until they start booking you for bacon campaigns to tell them that you are vegan. Make a list of things that you are comfortable and not comfortable doing. Common concerns for models are implied violence, nudity, alcohol, tobacco, and fur. This is a conversation about your morals, so you should not worry about being seen as difficult. You will be seen as more difficult if you keep turning down jobs without telling your agent why. And if your agent will not listen to you when you say that you are not comfortable accepting certain jobs, it is likely not the right agent for you.

Again, you do not need to sign with the first agency that offers you a contract. Don't be desperate. If a (reputable) agency is interested in you, it means that you are doing something right and another agency will see your potential as well. If you have something to offer the modeling industry, know your worth and don't settle for an agent that will not listen to your concerns.

***

Be your own advocate.

If your representation contract states that your agent or manager does not control the terms and conditions of services you provide or supervise your professional activities, it is incumbent upon you to provide your rep with your own terms and conditions so that you know what to expect on set, and your rep knows what is and is not acceptable to you. These terms can set out standards for your personal safety on set, overtime, meals, and more, depending on the job offer as presented to your rep.

Even if your rep doesn't ask for them in your agreement, have a standard set of your own terms and conditions that you can reference yourself. This way, when you are presented with an opportunity, you can make sure that the job aligns with your own expectations about on-set safety and similar issues.

Many models think that once they finally sign a management contract, it means that their manager will be on set with them overseeing the shoot. This is not the case. Recall that your model manager is most likely functioning as a booking agent, and booking agents do not have the capacity—or interest—to accompany you to set. If you have previously worked with a talent manager for film and television, your experience might certainly have been the opposite; sometimes talent managers do accompany talent to set. This is because while talent managers and model managers are both called "managers," they function very differently.

If you are working as a model, you must be aware that it is most likely the case that the only person on set looking out for your best interests is you. Because of this, you must be able to evaluate certain situations objectively, and if you need to take five minutes to call your agent or manager to ask him a question, you can politely excuse yourself momentarily to do so.

For example, if you show up to set and the photographer says to you, "I know that we agreed to do X, but I think we should also do Y," this can go in two directions. 1) This might be a great idea and something that you would be thrilled to do. But because it wasn't part of what your agency negotiated on your behalf, you should call your agent and run it by them first. If it is outside the scope of your original agreement with the client, your agency may be able to negotiate a bigger paycheck for you. Or, 2) this might be something that you are not sure that you should pursue, and might even sound a bit shady.

If you agreed to do a lingerie shoot but the photographer asks you to pose topless, call your agent even if you are perfectly comfortable with this. Any time you are presented with an idea that has not been previously discussed, call your agent. There should never be surprises on set, and while you can be flexible, you must remember that this is a business, that you are in control of your brand and image, and that you are the only person on set who is going to protect you fully. A lingerie shoot that turns into an artistic topless shoot may be fine under certain circumstances, but it also may be a sign that the photographer is taking advantage of you.

If you are shooting, say, a lingerie campaign and you have not contractually agreed to any nudity on set, do not remove your clothes even if the photographer tells you that the final image will not show anything. For example, a photographer might tell you that you will get a better shot if you pose nude, and that it will not be an issue because there will be artwork strategically placed over the final image so that nothing shows. Know that whenever you pose nude for a photo, there is a nude photo of you that exists in the world, and someone else has it in their possession, meaning you cannot control where it goes. Even if it is not published or released with malice, mistakes happen. If you do not want to be exposed, do not expose yourself.

If something seems off, or if something is presented to you that was not part of the original plan, get in touch with your rep. If they are unavailable, call your lawyer or career coach to run the idea by them. They may tell you that it is fine to proceed with just a quick contract update, or they may tell you to leave the set immediately.

Do not be concerned about coming across as difficult to work with. Your business is modeling, and you are acting professionally when you take the time to properly consider proposed business opportunities. And if you get a bad feeling about a certain individual or situation on set, excuse yourself from set. Remember that you can say no to anything and everything that makes you uncomfortable, and if you have previously communicated your dealbreakers with your agent, no one should try to pressure you into them.

What happens if it is not a photographer that seems off, but it is your agent that seems off? Then what do you do, and who do you call? There are two different situations that may arise here. First, you are meeting with a potential agent, and second, you are already signed with an agent.

If you have a meeting set up with a potential agent and he invites you to his apartment to have that meeting, you should immediately see this as a red flag. The agent might tell you that his office is being renovated, and that he works from home in a separate studio or office space in his apartment. This is not acceptable. If his office is being renovated and he has been temporarily displaced, he should suggest meeting in a public space, such as a coffee shop—and after you have met at this coffee shop, do not view that as a green light to then go to his apartment to see where he works. Do not go to his apartment at all, even if you think that you know him. Do not accept an invitation to dinner—this is a professional relationship and meeting for dinner may give him the wrong impression. If he even invites you to dinner, you should see this as a red flag.

If you are scheduled to meet with an agent in a foreign market and he offers you his guest bedroom so that you do not need to pay for a hotel, this is also a red flag. Even if you have been speaking with him on the phone, even if you have already met in person and think that you know him, do not stay in his apartment, and do see this also as a red flag. A reputable and professional agent will not offer his apartment to a potential client. All of this applies to both male and female agents, and male and female models.

If you are already in a situation where you are at a coffee shop, for example, already meeting with a potential agent, and something seems off, remove yourself from the situation immediately. You can be polite, but do not stay in a situation that could potentially take a turn for the worse. If you find that the situation already has turned and something happens to you—for example, the agent invades your privacy or personal space in an inappropriate manner, call your lawyer. If you are in a foreign country, go to your embassy to report the incident.

If you do not have a lawyer because you never needed one, set yourself up with one, even if you don't have an immediate issue or contract to review, so that you have someone at the ready to turn to if necessary.

One final point about advocating for yourself: Being your own advocate does not necessarily mean that you cannot participate in nude photoshoots, for example, if you wish to do so. Advocating for yourself means that for everything you choose to do, there must be a prior agreement that is adhered to, and when you show up to set there are no surprises. Modeling is indeed an art, but it is first and foremost your business.

The same principle applies to actors. Before you sign with an agent or manager, you should have a conversation about what you are and are not willing to do on camera. If you are comfortable taking on a role that requires nudity and "adult language" but not portraying a character that uses drugs, let your rep know. Let him know the degree of nudity that you are comfortable with, the circumstances (maybe you are fine with artistic nudity but not nudity in love scenes, for example), and let him know if it is a dealbreaker for you or if there are certain things that you will do only for an additional fee. Do not do things that you would not otherwise do, however, just for an additional fee. If you need extra money, talk to your agent about finding you "survival roles." Again, however, make sure that these extra roles do not overshadow or tarnish the reputation and image that you are trying to create in the industry.

Understanding the inner workings of the fashion, modeling, or entertainment industries is fundamental to understanding your rights as a model or actor. We have discussed various types of representation contracts, unions, and advocating for yourself as a professional in the business of acting or modeling. Now we will delve deeper into the various ways that you can establish yourself as a force in the industry, and additional ways to protect your personal brand.

BUSINESS

....

To have a successful modeling career, treat it like a business.

There is a difference between enjoying having your photo taken to post online and working in the industry as a professional model. If you have decided to pursue modeling professionally as a career, you need to treat it like a business in order to be successful. In fact, as previously discussed, you are the business, which means that you need to pay attention to your personal brand, your image, and your marketing, plus you need to consider all the behind-the-scenes factors—such as perhaps actually registering a company—that contribute to the success of that business. This can be as basic as always keeping your online presence updated, or as involved as making sure that the brands with which you work share your values and don't call your own personal brand into question.

Whether you are new to modeling or established, building your business will always be of paramount importance. Aside from your agent, manager, publicist, business manager, and anyone else that you might hire as your career grows, you should start working with a lawyer early to ensure that you are set up to properly manage your own business alongside your team. If you are set up properly from the outset, you will not need to scramble to get everything in place when you are already working steadily and do not have time to think about the organizational side of your personal brand.

There are a few administrative things that you should consider right away. First, consider whether you should start an LLC (limited liability company) for your acting and modeling services. This will be particularly helpful if you are also pursuing other business ventures in which your agent or manager is not involved. If you do not already have an LLC set up for your outside business ventures, consider how many LLCs you will need.

Ideally every large project will have its own LLC. This makes the most sense from both an accounting perspective and a legal/financial protection perspective. As a basic and simplified example, if you are a model but are also interested in producing films and you start a production company, each film should be produced under its own LLC even if it is branded as being a film produced by your production company (generally this requires filing a DBA, "doing business as," to keep your branding consistent). Say you have produced five films, each under its own LLC. If someone sees one film and for some reason brings a lawsuit, they will only be able to bring the lawsuit against the LLC associated with that film, not your entire production company.

On the other hand, you do not need separate LLCs for every acting and modeling job that you accept, since these are services that you provide for a client. The key word here is "services," which will be important when you file your LLC with the state in which you decide to establish your company. If you are an actor and model in Tennessee, for example, and you register an LLC in that state for your acting and modeling work, you will be considered as providing services and may or may not need a business license depending on how much money you earn from those services.

With acting in particular (but less so in modeling, as we have seen), sometimes you will be considered an employee of the production and sometimes you will not (on professional projects, you will generally be considered an employee). When you earn money from productions on which you are considered an employee, this income does not count toward the amount of income that would trigger the need for a business license in Tennessee. Each state has its own rules, but generally the registration process is similar.

Before you register your LLCs, however, you should determine exactly how many LLCs you will need, decide the state in which you would like to file (there are many factors that would go into this decision), and confirm that the LLC name is not already in use. Even if it is available for use in your state, also check whether the domain name and social media handles are available for use. This is, of course, not a legal requirement, but will be important for branding your business, and will also be helpful if you decide to trademark the name of your business in the future. And if, for example, mybusiness.com is not available but mybusinessllc.com is, you should probably go with a different name—no one is going to remember to type "LLC" when searching for your business website.

After you have decided on a name and your preferred state, you will file articles of organization for your LLC, get a federal tax ID number (an EIN), and get a registered agent. A registered agent will handle much of your business paperwork; for example, if someone sends you legal notices by mail, the registered agent will receive those notices and forward them to you. Again, each state has its own rules, but in many states your registered agent must be available at the address provided at all times during normal business hours. If you are thinking about naming yourself at your home address as the registered agent for your business, consider whether it makes sense for you to commit to being at home every day all day during normal business hours.

There will likely also be annual filing fees and other annual or biennial filings that you need to track. Mark these dates on your calendar, be sure that you have signed up for reminders, and consider whether you want to pay your registered agent to handle these filings for you as well.

Once you have your articles of organization and your EIN, you can set up your business bank account. A checking account will be the most useful for your business, and you should have checks printed as well as get a credit card. All business expenses should come out of your business account. If your business keeps a large sum of money in its checking account, you may not want to risk using a debit card for business purchases.

If you already work with an accountant, let him or her know that you have set up a new LLC, and figure out the best way to keep track of your business and personal income and expenses. Some people prefer to use software, but it is also very easy to keep a spreadsheet for yourself and manually itemize your expenses. Keep track of the expenses that you incur in your personal account while setting up your LLC before your business bank account is active, because those setup expenses should be considered business expenses. In your spreadsheet, make a note of this for your accountant.

Depending on the state, you may also need to publish a notice about your new LLC in one or more newspapers. This is generally not an extremely large expense, but you should budget for this, and also be aware that the business address will likely be published as well; so, if you were to use your home address as your business address, your home address would be published.

For your last bit of paperwork, you will need to submit a beneficial ownership information report. This is very simple and can be done online, as can most of the other steps outlined above.

Finally, if you are starting your LLC in a creative field, you should consider whether you need media liability insurance. Depending on your goals, there may be other specific insurance that you should look into as well, and as a general matter, both short- and long-term disability insurance may be a good idea.

After you have set up everything legally and have the necessary insurance in place, you still need to do more to protect your business and your brand. The easiest thing to do to get started is to buy website domains with your business name written in a variety of ways, including common or anticipated misspellings that you will redirect to your main site. For example, if your main business domain will be mytvbusiness.com, you should also claim mytelevisionbusiness.com, mytvbiz.com, mytelevisionbiz.com, etc. You may also want to claim .net versions of your website. Even if you don't plan to post on social media, claim the handles that make sense for your business, and if you have a logo, use that as your placeholder profile image. Solidifying your online presence is one way to try to protect your brand before you have filed a trademark—think of it as an online billboard.

Per your modeling contract, your image might be in the hands of your agent, but you are still in control of your brand. If you want to move your career in a certain direction, start curating that image. (This concept applies to your modeling portfolio as well; it should be forward-looking—not a collection of what you have done, but a glimpse into what your future modeling looks like.) Your agent only has access to the photos or content that you or the clients with whom you work provide to him. If you don't want something to be made public and you are not certain that your agent will respect your boundaries, don't give it to your agent—and also consider finding a new agent whom you can trust.

If you have already created content or products, you will want to make sure that you have filed the appropriate intellectual property ownership applications as well. If you cannot figure out if a trademark or a copyright filing applies to your work, consult a lawyer. Sometimes you need both for your creations to be fully protected, and sometimes only one or the other will apply.

If you are considering filing a trademark, there are a few things to know about trademark theory before you can understand trademark practice. Trademarks are meant to protect the consumer, not the brand. They are meant to signal authenticity to the consumer so that the consumer is not duped by imitations. For example, red soles on shoes signal to the consumer that they are buying Christian Louboutin shoes. Where Louboutin's trademark has been approved, any other non-Louboutin shoes with red soles are frauds created by bad actors trying to capitalize on the value that the red sole brings to a shoe. The purpose of granting the trademark is to signal to consumers that whenever they see a red sole, it is a true Louboutin. Louboutin must police his trademark and get rid of inauthentic Louboutins so that the consumer does not accidentally buy a pair of frauds.

In reality, some people seek out inauthentic, less-expensive versions of trademarked goods, so it would seem that owning a trademark is meant to protect a brand against losing its consumers to fraudsters. This is not the case. If Louboutin does not police the red sole trademark, he will lose it. In the eyes of the law, policing a trademark means removing inauthentic items from the market so that consumers are not confused.

Because the legal purpose of trademarks is "source signaling," meaning, a trademark indicates authenticity, the law looks to the consumer to determine what the authentic source is. For example, if two brands are competing for a trademark and brand 1 came into existence first but brand 2 is more popular, brand 2 will likely win the trademark battle because more consumers will associate brand 2 with the trademark in question. That is, the source signaled to consumers by the trademark is brand 2. This does not mean, however, that your brand must be famous before you will be granted a trademark, and like most things, whether or not your trademark application is approved somewhat depends on the person in the trademark office assigned to review your case.

Before thinking about approvals, however, you need to figure out what it is that you want to trademark, and in what spaces. If you have an unusual name, you may want to trademark it; even though a person's name is usually not permitted to be trademarked, an unusual name used in an unusual space may work.

If you have a color logo that includes your business name that you want to trademark, you will want to trademark the logo and the name separately. If you trademark them together as one image, when they are used separately, they will not technically be protected. So, you already have two trademarks to file. Although your logo is in color, think about whether you want to file a trademark in black and white as well as color—another two trademarks. What you might think is one trademark—your logo—may really amount to four trademarks to be fully protected.

Further, each trademark may have more than one class. A class is essentially a category of use. When you file a trademark, it does not offer blanket protection. If you were to file a trademark for a logo for a cosmetics line as well as a clothing line, the cosmetics and the clothes would be considered separate classes. Each class will require the payment of a filing fee. If you have already filed your trademark application for cosmetics and clothing and later you decide to use the same logo for a film production company, not only is that another class, but you will also need to file another complete trademark application.

There is a bit of a different process if your trademark is not already in use. Instead of submitting proof of use in commerce (for example, your cosmetics line is already in stores using the logo that you are trademarking), the application will state that you intend to use the trademark and you will submit proof of use in commerce a few months down the line (e.g., when your cosmetics line is finally launched). If you submit an "intent to use" application, you need to mark on your calendar when you will be submitting the completed application with proof of use so that you have time to prepare.

Before you start your application process, make a list—in order of priority—of what you want to trademark and in what spaces you plan to use that trademark so that you can budget appropriately.

***

Networking is not just socializing.

Aside from the administrative and organizational side of establishing yourself and your brand in the industry, you need to constantly be networking in order for your business (your business being you, as a model or actor) to succeed.

If you are a self-described introvert and the idea of networking terrifies you, train yourself to handle situations in which you need to walk into a room full of strangers. Think of it as part of your business—you are putting your professional self forward, not your personal self. Yes, this means that you need to be "on" whenever you are in public and this might be exhausting, so plan for personal time afterward.

You will need to get comfortable walking up and introducing yourself to strangers (and you will need this skill throughout your career). Eventually it will become a habit, and people tend to respond very well to it since it is so unusual for people to do. It shows that you are confident and open. After some practice you will be able to tell which "groups" of people you should not approach (for example, if there is a group standing in a close circle seemingly having a private conversation) and which ones will be more open to socialize.

If you are invited to an industry after-party, set goals for yourself. Aim to stay for thirty minutes and introduce yourself to two new people. You will probably find that you have stayed for about an hour before you are hit with social overload, and that you spoke to more than two new people because those two initial people introduced you to other people. Connect with the people you meet, don't just collect them.

Always keep your right hand free to shake hands so that you are not fumbling during introductions; don't carry a clutch bag in one hand and a drink in the other and expect things to go smoothly.

Plan in advance for certain likely situations. For example, if you keep business cards in a card case, make sure that the snap on the case is always partially open. This will ensure that you only need to use one hand to access the cards, and you won't accidentally have cards flying everywhere if the snap has gotten stuck before the case finally opened. Eliminate all the logistical stresses in advance so that you can focus on presenting the most polished and poised version of yourself. And yes, at the end of the evening, reflect on how you did.

A lot of introverts will reflect on their social interactions in a negative way. Be objective. Evaluate the logistical details first. Do you need to figure out how to hold a drink at the same time as you are holding a mini plate of food while keeping one hand free? (Answer: You can't. Pick one or find a table.) Do you need to remind yourself to hold your drink in your left hand so that when you shake someone's hand with your right hand it's not a cold, soggy handshake?

After you have evaluated the logistical details, move on to the substantive details. Do you need to refine what you say when you are ready to exit a conversation? Do you need to figure out what your go-to drink is in social settings, particularly if you don't consume alcohol? Don't ruminate, just debrief...briefly. If you have a career coach or manager, let him or her know how things went. And then put it out of your mind until you start preparing for your next event.

It may seem like overkill, but improving your networking skills will make you stand out, and it can be better for your business as a model or actor than the most flawless performance at a casting.

ETHICS

....

Clarify your own personal ethics for yourself.

Because the modeling industry is largely unregulated, models often do not know where to turn, and they view their agent as their protector. But agents are not always protective. It would be nice to be able to tell models to look at their agent as a business partner, and to look at a contract as an indication of how fairly they will be treated once they sign. If the agency puts clauses in the contract that aren't illegal but probably should be (and are definitely immoral), then it is a sign that the agency does not value the model appropriately.

Unfortunately, this is commonplace in the industry until models are more established and have more leverage—but to get to that point models often have to endure years of oppressive contracts, poor working conditions, and non-payment.

The entire modeling industry is currently running on inertia. Agencies will call themselves management companies, brands will book models as independent contractors, and everyone is happy except the models. And in many cases, the way the industry functions has become so institutionalized that agents and brands don't even know that there is an issue—they may have some general awareness that models speak out every so often about working conditions on set, but they don't realize that it is part of a larger issue.

Not only is no one overseeing and enforcing the laws governing agents and managers, but models are unable to form a union to ensure that they have protection because they are said to be independent contractors—another area of law that is not appropriately applied to the modeling industry.

The purpose of raising awareness about the ethical issues that pervade the modeling industry is not to take anyone down or shutter agencies altogether. The goal is to invite brands, agents, photographers, and other power players in the industry to treat models the way that they should be treated; it is not hard to treat people well. While we can certainly set our sights on policing the industry and creating stricter laws, the easier and less contentious thing to do would be to spread awareness about the issue and encourage self-regulation and self-reflection.

For example, if the same brands that purport to care about sustainability and garment workers' rights do not care about protecting models, then there is a disconnect and they must reevaluate their own brand's ethics.

There is a lot of discussion in fashion about sustainability and ethical treatment of garment workers, but there is not a lot of focus on protecting models. It is an open secret that models are often treated poorly and have few protections—even if brands work with only sustainable materials, improve working conditions and pay for garment workers, and achieve every other ethical goal they set for their company, they are still missing one fundamental group of individuals—the people who model their clothes.

Agents are likely to be the last group of individuals in the industry that will start acting more ethically because it does not immediately affect their bottom line.

But for brands, their image is at stake. It doesn't cost much for them to contribute to improving the industry for models, but it could be very costly if consumers start to turn away from their brand because they work with modeling agencies that exploit their models.

Some consumers disregard models because what they are generally exposed to are the rich, famous, glamorous models who don't seem to be struggling. But that is not the reality for most models (and rich, famous, glamorous models are not immune to mistreatment either). If consumers took the same ethical stance on models' rights that they do with sustainability, they could have an impact. We don't necessarily want to boycott brands, because it is not completely the brands' fault that models have this struggle, but we do want consumer voices heard.

Brands can start improving conditions for models by ensuring that the on-set working conditions at photo shoots are appropriate. They can have an on-set representative to ensure that the set conditions comply with their brand values—and this would apply to not only models, but to everyone working on that set. This would come at little cost to the brand, but would potentially have a huge impact, and it would ensure that their brand image, ethics, and reputation are consistent and flawless. They can stop working with photographers who don't respect models and stop working with agents who don't treat their models fairly. Small changes like this will not hurt a brand's bottom line, and will have a big impact on the modeling industry.

However, while it may be an open secret that models deal with these issues, figuring out who the perpetrators are means that someone needs to come forward, and often there are repercussions for models who come forward. A different approach would be to adopt a more positive stance rather than a negative one—encourage collaboration with agents and photographers who have a reputation among models for being excellent to work with. Instead of creating a blacklist, work on creating a "greenlist." It is more likely that models would be willing to come forward about positive experiences than negative ones, and slowly brands could start weeding out the bad actors that way.

Ideally brands would take these steps because it is the right thing to do and not use it for publicity. The reality is that brands will likely promote how well they treat their models. In this case, the positive side of that reality is that it also raises awareness about the issue.

It will take time for the industry to turn over completely, but being one of the first brands to actively take a stance on fair treatment of models is certainly not going to hurt their reputation. Models might stop being tempted to sign with disreputable agents if brands refuse to work with those agents, and things might slowly start falling into place from there.

Larger brands will have more leverage than fledgling photographers to take a stand against unfair treatment of models; they will be able to pick and choose the agencies and photographers with whom they work without losing much. A photographer who is trying to break into fashion is not necessarily in a position to say that he refuses to work with certain people because the reality is that he might need those people to get ahead in the industry.

We have seen that the laws that are in place are not enforced and are not clear. Imposing more laws that are not enforced, are not clear, or do not speak to the actual issues will not help to improve the modeling industry. Further, any new law that might be effective, responsive to the issues, and enforced would take too long to implement, and any enforcement would likely happen quietly, which would have no deterrent effect. There needs to be an understanding among the people and brands in positions of power that fair treatment of models is non-negotiable, and then it can flow down throughout the industry.

When we have this kind of dark secret weighing down the industry, we cannot possibly even know what we might be missing. How much talent has left the modeling industry because of its practices? How much more income could be generated for all parties if everyone were working toward a common goal instead of stepping on one party for an extra dollar? But maybe even more pressing is that it is hypocritical to boast ethical initiatives in certain areas and not in others, because it shows that there is only a superficial care about ethics and much of it is likely just performative.

This kind of performative action has also arisen in diversity initiatives that use AI models instead of real models—all this does is create the appearance of diversity while in reality it is eliminating opportunities for all models of all races. Or on runways that clearly cast one "plus-size" model for the sake of being able to say that the show features diverse body types. Or, on the flip side of that, demonizing size zero bodies. We have not yet realized that being a size zero does not automatically mean that a model is anorexic. We also have not yet realized, seemingly, that there are sizes in between a size four and a size twenty-four that can also be represented on runways. When we are too quick to act because we are concerned that not acting shows that we are not supporting diversity, we get it wrong.

To protect yourself in an industry that is as unregulated as modeling—in a society that has not yet figured out how to treat all humans with the same baseline respect without demonizing certain groups of individuals—you need to clarify for yourself your own personal ethics on a variety of topics.

Recall that sometimes agents will write in their contracts that they do not monitor or control what happens on set, and if something goes wrong they are not responsible. This means that if they book you for work with a photographer who tries to assault you, the agency will not get involved and you will need to handle the situation yourself.

When something like this does go wrong, how will you handle it? It may seem like an easy answer—of course, if someone gropes you on set, you will not tolerate that. But the reality is that when you are in these types of situations, you don't always know how to act. You might be on set with very powerful people in the fashion industry and be afraid to speak up—particularly if you are trying to get your foot in the door. You might be starstruck. You might not even realize that a line is being crossed until the situation is completely out of your control.

If you know that speaking up about abuse might mean the end of your career, will you remain silent? Will you accept mistreatment as you are building your name so that when you have a platform and a megaphone you can advocate for all models? Are you willing to walk away from an opportunity because someone is trying to take advantage of you?

At times, your only leverage will be your willingness to say no, knowing that "no" now does not mean that your career is over. If you are walking away from a bad situation—or even just walking away from an opportunity that seems fine but isn't quite right for you—you are not walking away from future opportunities; you are walking away from something that could potentially mean the end of your career. It is a long-term investment in yourself, and you must consider both the short-term and the long-term consequences of not walking away.

Prepare for a variety of situations. Think through hypotheticals. Talk with your career coach about possible delicate situations and how you might handle them. Most importantly, make sure that whatever your decision is, you are able to look at yourself in the mirror every day and know that you did what was right for you even if other people don't agree.

***

Be aware of how artificial intelligence will affect your work as a model.

With artificial intelligence becoming an increasingly large part of daily conversation, it may seem like AI can solve the perceived problem of needing more diversity in fashion. The idea is that generative AI can create renderings of diverse models that look good in a designer's clothes according to the specifications and opinion of the designer himself.

This may create equity, but it is an equity such that everyone is equally disadvantaged. Without diving too deeply into the topic or the distinction between equity and equality, if the point of diversity and inclusion is to give people opportunities who wouldn't normally have them, we cannot then take those opportunities away and give them to AI. That only creates the illusion of diversity, while disadvantaging both the people the Diversity, Equity, and Inclusion push was supposed to uplift as well as every other "group" of human models that are not largely considered historically disadvantaged.

In essence, this means fewer jobs for all models regardless of shape, race, creed, or gender. It also means fewer jobs for hair and makeup artists, casting directors, agents, managers, lawyers, photographers, and all other individuals whose jobs depend to some degree on the existence of human models. Like all technology, when used properly, AI can indeed be a great benefit. But when we rely on it so heavily that we neglect to consider the consequences or alternative solutions, it can become a great detriment.

On a more concrete level, AI has made certain modeling contracts more difficult to negotiate. The problem with contracts in general is that the drafters try to account for every possibility. The thinking is that if everything else is included in the contract but X is left out, then X must have been left out on purpose. In many cases, X was left out simply because the parties to a contract didn't think of it at the time of contract drafting. This will affect the interpretation of X issue in a dispute.

With AI in particular, not only is it difficult to plan for all potentialities, but it is difficult to plan for the potentialities that might be associated with technology that we cannot at present even imagine existing.

Further, the law often looks backward in order to move forward. That is, lawyers will look at existing contracts and cases to try to draft new contracts and argue new cases. Because AI is so new, lawyers have few resources to look back on to inform their current contract negotiations. It is trial-and-error, and the technology advances so quickly that lawyers need to find ways to protect their clients from as yet unknown potential issues that arise from technology that has not yet been developed. It requires creativity and linguistic mastery to specifically protect against unspecified pitfalls that only exist in possible worlds.

CASE STUDY

....

You have now been introduced to various laws and modeling contract issues, but it might be difficult to synthesize all the information and see how it would be put into practice. To illustrate a common issue and see how the laws apply to models, we will analyze a sample case.

Say that model M has signed an exclusive, three-year personal management contract with a New York modeling agency. It automatically renewed for another three-year term without her realizing, because she got busy with a family issue and hadn't marked the notice date on her calendar. Eighteen months into the new term, M realizes that she hasn't gotten paid for several modeling jobs that she worked over the prior two years. She reaches out to her agency, but they either ignore her or provide her only with vague accounting information or denials that they owe her any money. She presses them over the next several months as her financial situation becomes more dire, and the relationship with her agency sours. She decides that she no longer wants to work with the agency and receives an offer to model for another agency. She asks her agent to end their contract early, and lets the agent know that she would like to work with the other agency. The agent has the agency's lawyer contact M to communicate that the agency refuses to terminate the contract early. M becomes so frustrated with her agency that she wants to cut ties with them completely so that she can feel unburdened by their contractual link. She decides to leave the modeling industry altogether, and communicates this to her agent. The agent still refuses to terminate the contract. Knowing that she is stuck with the agent for at least another year, she tries to make the best of it and tells the agent that she is committed to continuing to work for her regular clients until the end of the contract term. She enjoys working with them and she needs the money.

In the meantime, M contacts a lawyer to see what her options are. She asks the lawyer whether she can argue that they cannot uphold their end of the bargain (getting her modeling jobs) if she has left the industry, which would result in a breach of contract.

There is more than one flaw in this argument, but we will focus on the main one that you as a model need to take away from this example. M believes that if her agency does not book her modeling jobs—and cannot book her modeling jobs—they will have breached the contract and she would then be free to work with another agency.

However, what the contract says does not reflect how the agency has functioned. It specifically says that it is not a talent or employment agent, that it is not licensed to procure work for M and does not agree to do so, and that it never indicated anything to the contrary to M in writing or in conversation. According to the contract, the agency's job is to advise

M on her career choices. M cannot argue that the contract was breached because the agency did not attempt to procure work for her when the contract specifically states that they will not do so.

What M can technically do is work with a true modeling agency. If the new modeling agency is licensed in a state where a license is required, or is not licensed in a state where a license is not required, the contract is more likely to accurately state that it is a modeling agency and will indeed endeavor to procure work for the model. Because M's New York agency contract says that it is an exclusive "personal management" (not agency) contract, M is free to sign with a model agent.

However, many model agents and managers don't know the legal, technical differences between the terminology used, and would be unwilling to sign M because she is with another modeling "agency."

One of the main problems with contracts generally is that while there may be laws on the books, it can be difficult to enforce them. Even if your contract is airtight, if someone breaks a promise, it may not be feasible for you to take legal action to try to right the wrong. Similarly, in modeling, while there may indeed be a way to bring legal action against unlicensed agents to free models from their contracts, most models do not have the time, energy, or money to do so. Further, most models do not want to risk being blacklisted from the industry by suing an agency for doing the very thing that most other agencies do.

If you are unhappy with your agency and wish to terminate your contract early, consult a lawyer. Your lawyer may advise you to just have a conversation with your agency first, but he or she will be able to tell you how to approach the conversation so that you are able to pursue other options if the agency is not receptive.

This case study is a brief illustration of how a simple contract term can cause complex practical issues for models. Using the knowledge you have gained about the business, law, and ethics of the fashion and modeling industries, you will be better able to understand how to avoid these types of situations yourself, but you should always remember to speak with a lawyer or career coach to help you navigate these issues.

What follows are checklists to help distill some of the information presented in this book, answers to some questions that you may have now that you have a better understanding of the industry, and additional tips to keep in mind.

CHECKLISTS

....

Forming an LLC

1) Determine how many separate LLCs you need.
2) Research whether the name is being used.
3) Decide in which state to establish your LLC.
4) File articles of organization.
5) Get a federal tax ID.
6) Sign up for a registered agent service.
7) Mark annual filing fee due dates on your calendar.
8) Set up a business checking account, and get checks and a credit card.
9) Contact an accountant and keep track of expenses associated with setting up your LLC that you pay from your personal account before the LLC is established.
10) Consider media liability insurance.
11) Look into disability insurance, long- and short-term.
12) Publish a notice in the required number of newspapers if your LLC was established in a state that requires it.
13) File the required Beneficial Ownership documents.

***

Branding

1) Determine what trademarks you need to file.
2) Determine what copyrights you need to file.
3) Buy relevant website domains.
4) Get social media handles.
5) Google yourself and update or remove anything necessary where possible.
6) Cleanse your social media accounts, both public and private.
7) Make sure that your website is updated.

***

Things to discuss with your agent in advance about what you are and are not willing to do on set

1) Nudity
2) Implied nudity
3) Implied violence or abuse
4) Lingerie
5) Swimwear
6) Alcohol
7) Smoking
8) Implied drug use
9) Implied sex
10) Wearing real fur
11) Working with unethical brands
12) Promoting only sustainable fashion
13) Eating certain foods due to allergies

14) Specific types of products that you do not want to promote, such as energy drinks, supplements, tampons, etc.

***

Basic contract points to note

1) Type of contract (model management, talent management, personal management, booking agent, mother agent)
2) Initial term length
3) Exclusivity
4) Auto-renewal period
5) Termination clause
6) Notice requirements
7) How long does a client have to pay the agency, and how long after that does the agency have to pay you
8) Representation fields/scope of representation
9) Mother agency clause in original booking agent or model management contract
10) Advance payment terms
11) Expenses list
12) Collections procedure and payment responsibility
13) Mandatory arbitration clauses
14) Terms that include language such as "in their sole discretion," "in perpetuity," "worldwide," "throughout the universe," "costs borne entirely by talent/model," and "not yet conceived"

***

Common red flags

1) An agent or manager asking for a meeting in his or her apartment or house
2) An agent or manager offering you a room in his or her home to sleep in if you are traveling
3) Anyone asking for sensitive bank account details so that they can "reimburse" you for costs
4) A photographer who pressures you to do something on set outside the scope of your contract, particularly if there is no one else on set with you
5) Individuals with no online presence whatsoever
6) Agents who say that they will pay for your travel expenses and paint a picture of a glamorous lifestyle
7) Agents who ask for money up front for things like mandatory photo shoots, acting classes, or runway coaching
8) Agents, managers, photographers, or other professionals who advise you against consulting with a lawyer
9) Agents or managers who pressure you to sign a contract before you have time to review it with a lawyer
10) Agents or managers who use their "legal team" as an intimidation factor

11) Photographers who cannot or will not provide references
12) Sudden photo shoot location changes of which your agent was not made aware
13) Photographers who refuse to allow anyone else on set
14) Individuals who claim to be agents from a reputable agency but do not have an official agency email
15) An agent or manager who says that you must emancipate your child as a condition of the representation offer

....

*What say should a model have on how much money an
agency spends on her behalf?*

You should always have complete control over
your finances, and should also be fully aware of every
cent that is earned and spent. Modeling contracts
often contain language that goes against this, and you
will likely need to change some of the terms that give
your agency control. When you are offered a modeling
contract, make sure that you fully understand the
financial terms. Look for words like "expenses,"
"advances," and "reserve account."

You can certainly give your agency reasonable,
limited control that allows for them to book you and
pay you more efficiently, but they should not be given
free rein to spend your money with no limits, and you
still need to keep track of what they spend. Also,
remember that even though you may understand the
plain English, the words may take on a different
meaning in a legal context or when read together with
the rest of your contract terms.

***

What happens to any money owed to or by a model when leaving an agency?

When you leave an agency, whether because your contract came to its natural end or it was terminated early by either you or your agent, all money that is owed to you by your agency and all money that you owe to your agency becomes due. Your contract will usually specify a deadline for making these payments, and that deadline is usually "immediately," though some contracts allow for a generous seven days.

What is important to remember here is that your agency usually has the right to terminate your contract at any time. If your agency has advanced you money for work-related expenses and later terminates your contract before you are out of debt, this can leave you in financial trouble.

Think about it this way: If you had the money to reimburse your agency immediately for those advances, you should have just paid for those expenses yourself from the outset. If your agency had to advance you money, it was presumably because you did not have the money to pay for those expenses yourself. So, unless your financial situation changed after your agency advanced you money, you could be in some trouble. It is not necessarily the case that all expenses will be covered in full after you are paid by a client, and this is also why it is important to keep track of your finances and consider whether certain jobs are worth the expense.

Remember that your agency does not pay for expenses out of its own pocket—you pay—but your agency will always earn its 20% commission. So even if a job nets you no money or even leaves you in the red, your agency will still make money. It is up to you to determine whether accepting a job is going to be financially beneficial, either in the short-term or in the long-term, by building your portfolio so that you can book higher-paying jobs. If you take a job with an eye toward long-term career building instead of short-term financial gain, be careful about how much money you allow your agency to spend on that portfolio-building opportunity.

***

Can an actor/model have both a talent manager and a model manager?

If you are both an actor and a model, you can have both a model manager and a talent manager provided that neither manager's contract states that it is an exclusive personal management contract in all fields. If you are offered personal management contracts by both managers, you need to specify the fields—your talent manager will manage your film/TV acting work, and your model manager will manage your modeling work in fashion. Figure out which manager will handle your on-camera commercial work, as this is an area that will overlap.

Remember that this issue arises because most managers are not actually personal managers, but function instead as booking agents. The terminology is important because standard industry practice is sometimes not fully in line with what the law permits.

***

What should models do when they want to get out of an agency contract early?

Most modeling contracts do not explicitly allow for the model to terminate the contract early, and agents will tell you that this is okay because if something isn't working they won't want to hold you on their roster. This is true in certain situations, but you cannot rely on this. If you want to terminate your contract early, you have a few options.

First, try to have a conversation with your agent. It is always better to have these discussions in person if possible, because the tone of emails can be misinterpreted and immediately put the agency on the defensive, which might make your agent less likely to entertain the thought of letting you out of your contract early. It may be scarier to have difficult conversations face-to-face, but it is more likely to give you the result that you want without spoiling the relationship.

If you have a career coach, mentor, or lawyer, you should consult with him or her first to plan what you will say to your agent; many models overshare when they are nervous to have this conversation, and sometimes it leads to the agency holding the model to the contract.

Sometimes a simple conversation will work—particularly if the agency has not been able to find you jobs. When the relationship isn't working for either of you but there still remains a mutual respect, the agency is more likely to agree to let you out of the contract early.

If the relationship has soured or if you are working with an agent who doesn't want to give you the opportunity to move to a competing agency, it will be more difficult to break your contract early.

Many models think that if an agent hasn't gotten them work or has "benched" them (i.e., the model might work if the agency tried to book them, but the agency is holding them on their roster and is not actively looking for work for them—and may even be turning down available work for them if the relationship has gone particularly south), that the agent has breached the contract and they can terminate it early.

Recall that most modeling contracts will state that the agent is "not an agent," does not agree to procure work for the model, and did not tell the model otherwise. All of this is untrue, but it means that you cannot claim that the agency breached the contract by not procuring modeling work for you—it says right in the contract that they will not do this.

There are other potential options for terminating your contract early; these options will depend on the specific language your contract uses, and will require a lawyer to evaluate.

**

Do modeling agencies pay for a model's work-related
expenses?

No! Remember that even if an agent paints a
glamorous picture and claims that the agency will pay
for your plane tickets, hotels, meals, and cars, they
don't mean that they will pay out of their own
pocket—they will either advance money to you that
you need to pay back, or they will take the money out
of your reserve account (which is 100% comprised of
your money), so you are technically paying for your
own expenses anyway. Plus, if they use money from
your reserve account to pay for your expenses, you
will likely need to replenish your reserve account
before you see any money earned from future
modeling jobs.

So, essentially, not only are you paying for
your own expenses, but you won't see your future
earnings until you replenish your reserve account.
You will have more money in your pocket at any given
time if you pay for your own work-related expenses
instead of allowing your agency to advance any money
or hold any money in a reserve account.

**

If a model has both a manager and a mother agent, does she
give up 30% in commission?

No again! As long as your contracts provide for this scenario—as they should—you will still only see 20% of your gross earnings taken out in commissions. This is usually split between your manager and your mother agent, such that they each get 10%.

The way this works is that you will have a contract with your mother agent as well as a contract with your model manager. Your model manager and your mother agent will also have a contract between themselves. You won't be a part of their contract, and you likely won't even see it, but it will state that the model manager will pay the mother agent half of what it takes in commission from you. So, your model manager first takes 20% commission, then pays you the remaining sum. For example, if you earned $1,000.00 (gross), your model manager would take $200.00 and pay you $800.00. Of that $200.00, your manager would keep $100.00 and give your mother agent $100.00.

Whether or not you have a mother agent when you sign with a model manager, your management contract should contain a mother agency clause. If you sign with a mother agent before you sign with a model manager, your mother agency contract might say that you owe your mother agent the full 20% commission, but it should also specify what the commission split will be once you sign with a manager.

Usually mother agents operate properly even if their contract does not specify what happens once you sign with a manager, but you still want to make sure that your mother agency contract contains the right language. Otherwise, you technically could be responsible for continuing to pay your mother agent the full 20% commission once you sign with a model manager.

***

Does a model have the right to dictate what type of work he or she is comfortable with?

Yes, but this does not mean that you can show up to set and say, "I am not comfortable wearing red because I think it's a terrible color on me." First, if red were a terrible color on you, the client would not have booked you for a job that requires you to wear red—no client wants a model to look terrible when marketing their products. Second, if you don't want to be seen as difficult, you should communicate what work you are and are not comfortable with before your agent tries to book you for those kinds of jobs.

The type of work you are comfortable with is a moral decision. Refusing certain jobs due to morals does not make you difficult to work with, but again, have this conversation in advance. If you forgot to mention something and your agent brings you a job that you are not comfortable with, let him know that you will need to decline the offer and also that he should not try to book you for such work in the future.

Similarly, refusing certain jobs due to image or branding concerns is also permissible. These types of decisions are more case-by-case than blanket moral decisions, so you may need to discuss these jobs with your agent as they arise and determine whether they might help or hinder your long-term career goals.

Refusing a job because you don't like the clothes is a different story, and is only acceptable in extremely limited circumstances. Here again, talk to your agent.

***

Why isn't there a union for models?

Employees, not independent contractors, can form a union. Recall that models are generally considered independent contractors. You might think that models and actors engage in a similar type of work and would be classified in the same way—actors are considered employees, usually of the production company to which they are providing their acting services, and models should be considered employees of the client for whom they are modeling. However, in an industry with so little oversight, whether there are practical differences between the type of services actors provide and that which models provide has not been deeply analyzed or discussed.

Your modeling contract likely states that you are an independent contractor. However, it is not up to the parties to decide whether you are an independent contractor or an employee. Again, there are certain factors that determine whether you are an employee—and many of these factors in reality point to models looking more like employees than independent contractors.

The more awareness there is surrounding these types of issues, the more likely it is that models will in the future be considered employees. At that time, they would be able to form a union.

If we look more deeply into it, models would not necessarily even need to form a union if they were generally treated more fairly. But the industry power players have demonstrated that they cannot self-regulate in an ethical manner, which means that the protections a model union would provide are critical.

***

Who owns the copyright when a model is photographed?

It would take another book to adequately explain copyright law, but the important thing to remember is that copyright law has not kept up with technology, including the rise of social media. This makes it difficult to determine what the law actually is and how it applies to certain situations. Every time a court makes a decision about a case, it clarifies the existing laws and brings them slightly more up-to-date, but this is not a quick or thorough process.

What the law currently says is that the person who takes the photograph automatically owns the copyright; it is not necessary to actually file for copyright protection to be protected—filing offers different kinds of protection (including proof of copyright ownership and monetary compensation if your copyright is infringed), but you as a creator already own the copyright automatically as soon as you create a work.

Based on existing laws, if a model substantially contributes to the creation of the photograph, the copyright ownership might be shared between the photographer and the model. Note that "substantially contributes" means more than posing for the photo— it means contributing things like ideas for the entire concept, the atmosphere, the mood, etc., but there is no exhaustive list to consult. Normally this is not the case when you are working as a professional model, and the photographer will own the copyright.

However, because it is a photograph of you, the photographer needs your permission to use the photograph for commercial purposes. This is why you will usually be handed a "model release" form to sign. (What your model release says will depend on whether you hired the photographer to take specific photographs of you or you were hired to model for a client.) If you do not give this permission, the photographer will be limited in how he can use the photograph.

Be careful when you sign model release forms—these should be given to you in advance and not when you arrive to set. In some cases, models have signed forms without reading them first, and were subsequently unable to even add the photos to their portfolio.

***

Why don't New York modeling agencies represent minors anymore?

They do—however, the laws have changed and it has affected how agencies treat their underage models.

In short, underage models are now treated the same way as child actors, meaning that there are new requirements and restrictions on working with underage models that were not previously in place. These requirements and restrictions are slightly more burdensome for clients—if a client can book an eighteen-year-old model who looks sixteen instead of booking a sixteen-year-old model who looks her age, the client will book the former.

While it is not impossible to work as an underage model, agencies know that they will likely book underage models less due to these new laws in New York. So, while they do still offer contracts to underage models, it is with the understanding that there may be a long "development" period until the model turns eighteen. Because agencies generally don't make money unless their models work, some New York agencies have started to cut back on how many underage models they sign.

***

What are the first steps to take to start a career as a model?

The first step is to educate yourself about the industry. Because there are so few resources that are transparent about the inner workings of the industry, try to find a career coach or consultant who will walk you through the process. You should speak with them regularly.

Think of it like you would think of an acting class. If your acting class meets once per week for eight weeks, you will learn during class and then will be given things to work on outside of class. Then during the next class, you will review what you worked on outside of class, and will be given a new set of things to work on before the next class. A step-by-step process with regular meetings will be the most efficient and effective way to get you started in your career and to keep advancing.

On a practical level, whether you are brand new to modeling or you are experienced in one type of modeling and want to move into another type of modeling, you need to have basic images. Before you even start thinking about building a portfolio, make sure that you have strong digitals that you update whenever your appearance changes. Often when you have strong digitals you don't even need a portfolio for an agency to express interest in signing you. Review these digitals—as well as your submission email—with your career coach or consultant first to have the best chance of presenting yourself well.

***

When can a model start getting paid for work and stop doing work for trade?

In general, you should start getting paid for your work when you have something to offer. In order to get to this place, you will likely first need to work for trade. This means, for example, working with photographers who are also trying to build their own portfolio. No money is exchanged, but you both get value out of the shoot. You don't want to get stuck here, however, and do want to make sure that you work with photographers who are going to produce usable portfolio photos—otherwise it may not be worth your time.

In the modeling industry, even when you are well-established there are many jobs that will be unpaid that you will take simply because it is great for your book (portfolio) or because it is a great opportunity to work with someone in particular. You should not dismiss these opportunities simply because they are unpaid, but you do need to balance them with paid work.

Early-career models who are unrepresented often don't know how to set their modeling rate. There are no defined steps to guide you; that is, for example, there is no rule that says that after you've appeared in five independent magazine editorials you can start charging for your time. Your rate will depend on many factors and may vary per job depending on the type of work. If you are unrepresented and are worried about setting your rate too high or too low, talk with other models or your career coach.

There is sometimes a lot of pressure by agencies to keep modeling rates quiet, but in an industry that is so highly unregulated, models should have an open dialogue with each other, and this dialogue should include rates.

Think of it this way: If there were a model union, there would likely be a minimum rate set for a variety of jobs. This rate would be public knowledge, and models would not be pressured to keep their rates secret. The more light shed on every aspect of the industry, the better it will be for models individually and collectively.

Sometimes mid-career models will continue to work for free not because they need more portfolio images, but because they enjoy the work. This is fine to an extent, but if you do it too often it sets a precedent. And if you have been freelancing as a mid-career model and are looking for an agency, agencies will want to see that you are able to earn money, not just that you work consistently on unpaid gigs.

In short, it depends. But before you start charging clients, make sure that you bring something to the table. And when you get to that point, make sure that you are fairly compensated for the value that you bring.

***

How can a model maintain a long career in the industry?

This answer, like many parts of this book, applies to both models and actors. The critical takeaway is that you must have the right people on your team. You need to remember that your career is ultimately yours to control—no one can dictate or force you to do anything if you are properly protected. Knowing who should be on your team comes with experience, and until you have that experience, talk things through with someone you trust—a parent, a friend, someone else in the industry—simply hearing your own thoughts said out loud sometimes makes you realize something that you wouldn't otherwise have realized.

Many actors work with both an agent and a manager early in their career. Sometimes they realize later that they only need an agent. And sometimes they realize that it is not a talent manager that they need, but a personal manager, because they want to expand their career opportunities from film and television roles to starting a cosmetics line. The types of people on your team will depend on your goals, but you will always need to look at the people on your team as individuals beyond their title and see if they are right for you.

More practical ways to maintain a long career include networking. Be kind to everyone—and not just because you want something from them. Be professional. Be someone that people want to work with—usually people want to work with people that they just want to be around generally. You have probably heard that in entertainment or fashion, it is all about who you know. It is actually not about who you know—it is about who knows you. As soon as you step outside of your private, personal space and into a public space, you need to embody the image that you are trying to project. And even when you think that you are in your personal space—say, you maintain a private, personal social media account for friends and family separate from your public-facing professional account, you must remember that anyone can take a screenshot of something that you have posted and share it publicly. Online, nothing is private.

***

How do models deal with constant rejection?

First, figure out if you are being rejected for good reasons. If your portfolio needs improvement or if your submission letter is full of spelling errors, you are going to have a harder time moving forward. If you work with a career consultant and your entire "package" is polished and flawless, then you need to remember that the only thing that you cannot control or predict is timing. It may be that an agency loves your look but already has someone on their roster like you. This doesn't mean that you cannot apply to that agency again; models change agencies, agencies expand and cut their rosters, and clients look for different things depending on the season.

If you remain prepared and persistent, eventually you will advance. This does not mean that you will suddenly be signed with the best agency, or even that you will start working right away. The markers of advancement often pass by unnoticed. Regulate your expectations of success, be persistent, and remind yourself that rejection is part of the industry—it is business, not personal, and it doesn't necessarily mean that you are doing anything wrong.

***

Are non-exclusive agencies lower quality?

Not necessarily. Depending on the market, non-exclusive agencies might be the norm. However, do not sign with a non-exclusive agency thinking that it will leave you completely free to sign with any other agency; if you are already signed with an agency, even if non-exclusively, it might deter other agencies from signing you because those other agencies may indeed require exclusivity.

***

What is the difference between a fashion lawyer, a model lawyer, and an entertainment lawyer?

In general, fashion lawyers tend to focus more heavily on the brand side, including trademarks. Model lawyers focus more heavily on model protections, which may include intellectual property, contract negotiations, contract termination, payment issues, and more issues that models in particular commonly face. Entertainment lawyers generally focus more on film/TV/theater production contracts, film/TV talent management contracts, and similar. Sometimes fashion law is considered to be a small part of entertainment law, and model law is considered to be a small and obscure part of fashion law. But in practice, they are distinct and require a different set of particularized knowledge, though they are indeed related.

***

Why would a model/actor work with a career consultant/coach if he is already working with a manager?

Actors will often start working with a manager before they begin working with an agent. And when they are given a management offer, they sometimes don't have any other offers on the table, so they will sign with that manager. A career consultant can help determine whether that manager is the right manager for the actor, and how to move a seemingly stagnant career forward. Further, consultants usually do not work on commission, so they are in a better position to offer more objective advice about what roles an actor should take and how an actor should brand himself. Many managers push actors into roles or "types" that they know will pay more, but that the actor doesn't want to play.

As an actor/actress, you may not even need a manager if you are already working with an agent, because often—like in modeling—managers book jobs more than they give career advice.

Models are different because most model managers are actually functioning as booking agents. This means that even if a model has a "manager," they may not have anyone on their team at all giving them career advice.

***

Doesn't SAG regulate managers?

SAG does not regulate or oversee managers in any way. No one does, and this is part of the problem. Even though we do have some laws in various states that are supposed to regulate managers, no one really monitors to make sure that those laws are enforced.

***

What if I signed my contract without reading it?

If you signed a modeling contract without reading it, all hope is not lost. Sometimes model agents or managers will hand you a contract and encourage you to sign immediately. And, as we've seen, a lot of models do because they feel intimidated by the agents waiting for them to sign, or they think that the agency has their best interests at heart and therefore the contract is probably fine. Or sometimes they think that getting a lawyer involved is a bit dramatic.

Whatever the reason, many models sign representation contracts without a second thought, and then later they feel trapped or confused. If you don't feel like you currently have any issues with your agency, that's great; you should still talk about the contract with a lawyer to make sure that you understand what everyone's obligations are. You might find that you could be getting more out of your contract than you already are. Sometimes the terms don't mean what you might think they mean, and you could potentially be leaving opportunities untapped. Or there may be some things that you need to watch for in the future that aren't causing you trouble right now so you don't think there is anything wrong.

If you do feel like you are having issues with your agency, it doesn't necessarily mean that the only option is to try to terminate the contract. You might be able to renegotiate more favorable terms.

Even if you already have a signed contract, and even if things seem to be going well, you can—and should—have the contract reviewed by a lawyer.

***

How can I afford a lawyer when I haven't even started working as a model yet?

No matter what creative industry you are in, you need to make sure that you have your own "legal savings egg." Actors, models, musicians, designers, and everyone outside of creative industries all need to have their own personal legal insurance. This means that every week you should put some money aside for potential legal fees. It does not need to be a lot of money; choose a number that makes sense for you, but be consistent. If you put aside $10.00 a week, that's fine. Make it a habit, so that when you are tempted to not put that money away, you will feel strange about it. If you can't save $50.00 a week, don't. Save $20.00. Consistency is the most important thing. Don't think about it once you've put it away.

Over time you will have a good amount of money set aside in case you do need a lawyer. Let's say that a talent manager wants to sign you but you don't have the $500.00 it will cost to hire a lawyer to negotiate your contract. Down the line you realize that your contract gives your intellectual property rights to your manager—basically meaning that anything you create your manager owns and controls. Now you need to spend way more than $500.00 to hire a lawyer to fight the consequences of this.

What happens before the signatures can be very smooth and not horribly expensive. What happens after the signatures can be much more adversarial and costly in many ways. You want to take advantage of the opportunity you have before the signatures happen to try to avoid everything that can fall apart after the signatures happen. And to do that you need to set yourself up with a reasonable legal savings plan.

QUICK TIPS FOR MODELS AND ACTORS

....

A few final bits of advice:

1. Legal fees are not the place you want to start cutting costs. Invest in your career, and not just in the things that you can see. If you would pay for acting classes, headshots, and test shoots but not a lawyer, you are doing yourself a disservice. Unlike agents and managers who usually take a percentage of your gross pay, lawyers generally do not. Certainly it is harder to pay money out to someone when you've seen it come in than it is to never see it come in at all. But if you are keeping track of your finances the way that you should be, the commissions that your representation takes will seem like real money to you in the same way that legal fees will. Budget, put it aside in savings every week as previously suggested, and it will be as if it never came in.

2. If you are a freelance model, you need to have your own contracts with each of your clients, photographers, and any other collaborators or

business partners. You can create a template with a lawyer and adjust it per client.

3. If you have a referral from someone for anything that you do in the entertainment or modeling industries, you are more likely to be treated better by the person to whom your contact introduced you.

4. If you receive an agency contract with no logo or an email with no signature, take extra care to verify that the person with whom you are communicating is actually from the agency. A lawyer can help you figure this out, and it does not need to be costly.

5. If you are offered a contract from a foreign agency that is written in two languages, know that the foreign language usually prevails if there is a discrepancy between the English version and the foreign language version. Further, automatic online translations are not sufficient to ensure that the translation is accurate. Again, sometimes words take on a different meaning when applied in a legal context, and sometimes automatic translations are literal and don't capture the real meaning of the words. Even if the word is properly translated, the legal meaning may not come across.

6. If a photographer has agreed to delete a photo of you that was taken during a shoot, make sure that it is deleted from the trash as well.

7. Don't leave it to your agent to get you jobs or your manager to make introductions. Continue

to find opportunities for yourself, and keep your reps up to date. Ask your manager to make specific introductions that make sense for you. Create your own content.

8. If you receive an email that contains important information that you might rely on in the future for legal purposes, save it as a PDF on your computer. Things happen, and emails disappear. This is one way to back up.

9. Read every draft of your contract. If you are negotiating a contract alongside your lawyer, every draft that is returned to you with updates needs to be read over in full—not just the pieces that were updated—to make sure that no other changes were made either sneakily or inadvertently.

10. Never let other people in fashion or entertainment know how much you don't know. You will be preyed upon.

11. Time your communications, and consider time zones. Generally it is not wise to send emails on Friday afternoon or Monday morning. On Friday, if your email isn't urgent, it will likely be ignored until Monday, and by the time Monday comes around, your email will be buried underneath a pile of other emails. On Monday morning, everyone needs to catch up and get themselves organized for the week, so adding to the barrage of tasks won't help.

12. If someone says that their contract is non-negotiable, call them. Usually once the person

is on the phone, the contract magically becomes negotiable.

13. Sometimes you need to spend time undoing things in order to move forward. You might find that when you start working with a career consultant or coach, it seems like you are going back to basics and tearing things down that you've built. Most of the time this is to "declutter," not to "undo," so that you can present only the best version of your personal brand. It won't take long to do this, but it is very worthwhile.

QUICK TIPS FOR AGENTS AND MANAGERS

....

The idea is to find nirvana between models and agents. The relationship between models and their representatives does not need to be adversarial, and much of the relationship can be improved by making small changes that don't cost time or money.

1. In your agency-client agreements, include a clause that makes it clear that if your agency needs to pursue the client for non-payment, either legally or through a debt collector, the client will be responsible for the associated costs. Most agency contracts make this the model's responsibility. Most models cannot afford this, and you cannot get blood out of a stone. So even if you thrust this responsibility onto your models, you will likely not be able to recover the money you are owed. And if your clients do not want to agree to this term, it might be an indication that they anticipate not being able to pay.

2. You want to be free to work in your business, not on your business. This means that you want to do as little administrative work as possible so that you can focus on booking

your models. So many of the issues models and agents have are administrative, e.g., a model doesn't understand why she was charged for new comp cards or two Uber rides instead of one. Instead of advancing money to models, have them pay for their own expenses. Tell models that you need new comp cards for them and have them print and send them to you. Don't deal with invoices and expenses and accounting more than you need to, and it will reduce the number of emails you receive from models disputing expenses.

3. Mother agents: Make it clear to models how you will work with subagencies. Many models think that if they work with a mother agent, they will be giving up 30% commission (10% to the mother agent and 20% to the subagent). Tell the models that you have a separate contract with subagencies and will be splitting a total of 20% commission.

4. Acknowledging the existence of "facsimile" but not "email" means that you are using old language from outdated contracts. Technology changes, industry practice changes, and the law changes. Review and update your contracts on a regular schedule (e.g., during slow seasons) to ensure that your business and your working relationships with clients and models stay protected. You should have at least three basic types of contracts always updated and ready for use: agent-model, agent-client, agent-mother agent.

5. If models aren't signing your contract, it's because the contract is overkill. For mother agents, make sure that the language in your contract actually belongs in your contract and not in a booking agency contract. For agents, don't try to force a model to be accompanied by an agent to a doctor if she is ill. This is too much. If you don't trust your models to tell you when they are sick, there are deeper issues in your relationship. If a model is constantly sick and backing out of work, have a conversation. Put other provisions in the contract that protect against no-shows and late cancellations, but don't invade her health privacy.

FINAL THOUGHTS

··

A lot of people in the modeling and entertainment industries will try to tell you as a model that you don't need a lawyer. Agents may tell you that it is not worth it because they have your back. Other models might tell you that you don't need a lawyer because their experience with their agency has been great, they never needed one, and lawyers are too expensive, scary, and stubborn. Photographers might pressure you to do something that is not in your contract and tell you that you are wasting time if you don't immediately agree. And even if no one is telling you that you don't need a lawyer, you might think to yourself that with all the other expenses you have, you cannot afford a lawyer, and the contract seems pretty clear to you so there is really no point in having a lawyer review it.

Even if not a single term is ultimately changed in a contract, it is worth consulting with a lawyer so that you understand what your contract says. Some agencies say that contracts are non-negotiable but will end up negotiating, and some agencies say that they are non-negotiable and ghost you if you try to ask questions about it. If you decide to sign with an agency that will not budge on their contract, you still need to understand what you are signing and take note of certain provisions that might trap you in the contract for a longer period of time than you realize.

Some words mean something different in plain English than they do in a legal context, so even if you understand what is on the surface, the effect of the words might mean something that you could not possibly anticipate.

Further, contracts are not only about what is contained within them, but what is left out. If you are a model and are handed a representation contract, you are immediately at a disadvantage because you are not the person who drafted the contract. The agency may have strategically left out certain words or phrases that you might not think about when you are reading the contract for comprehension.

Additionally, the terms in a contract cannot be read as standalone terms. They must be read in the context of the contract as a whole because they interact with each other. Even if you understand the terms individually, you may be missing critical points.

This is also why AI legal jargon translators cannot replace a lawyer looking over your contract. New technology uses artificial intelligence to translate legal jargon in contracts into everyday terms that are easy to understand. This might seem like a good idea at first, but this will likely result in many models signing bad contracts because AI cannot translate terms that are missing from contracts that should be included, and AI cannot tell you how the terms will affect you in reality within the context of the modeling industry.

If you consider how much money you spend as a model or an actor on headshots, test shoots, commissions, printing costs, classes, etc.—which are all recurring expenses—you should consider that occasional legal fees are necessary to protect those other investments. If you are trying to budget, the last thing you should cut out is legal fees. Hiring a lawyer from the outset can save you a lot of money in the future when you realize that you are in a bad contract and want to get out of it.

If you have a mother agent, you might be told that you do not need a lawyer because your mother agent will review your contracts for you. A mother agent cannot replace a lawyer. Lawyers are generally better able to interpret the reply of an opposing party because of the type of professional training they receive. Not all lawyers are of the same caliber, but if you find a good one, he or she will be able to read between the lines.

For example, say a model knows that her contract auto-renewed, but she wants to leave her agency and doesn't know the exact month that she can leave. She asks her agent for a copy of her contract and is very politely told that the agency will send it to her the following day. A week later the model follows up, and follows up again in another week. After several emails to her agent, the model finally receives a rude response from the agent stating that if it were that easy to just send, they would have sent it to her already. A lawyer might see this as an opportunity. This tells the lawyer that the agency cannot find the contract. The model can go ahead and give her agency notice of termination; then if the agency says that she has six months left on her contract, the model asks the agency to show her the provision in the contract that states this. They will then either need to produce the contract, or let her out of it because they cannot show that it is too soon for her to terminate. The latter is more likely since it will be too much work for them to argue a contract point contained in a missing contract.

Even if your mother agent sees modeling contracts all the time, she could be making the same mistake with every single contract. For example, say there is a model who loves and trusts her mother agent. The model's mother contacts a lawyer to look over a booking agency contract even though the mother agent said that it was fine to sign and the model does not want to go through a lawyer. The lawyer finds a buried provision that states that if the model does not answer her phone immediately, she would need to pay the agency for potential lost earnings. The mother agent may not think to define the term "immediately," but the lawyer would. This is not an uncommon issue with some mother agents, and this is not an uncommon buried clause to find in booking agency contracts.

Good intentions—while the modeling industry could certainly use more of them—are not always enough. A good mother agent will guide a model and direct the model to experts when needed. And if a mother agent is not also a lawyer, a separate legal expert needs to be added to the model's team.

ABOUT THE AUTHOR

Kaitlin Puccio is a lawyer and bioethicist. She is the founder of Puccio Law PLLC where she focuses heavily on modeling law, as well as Bent Frame Agency, a career consulting firm for individuals in fashion/modeling, entertainment, and media. She holds a JD from Georgetown Law and an MS in bioethics from Columbia University. She was formerly a model.

For the Insight video series, visit www.pucciolawpllc.com/insight